I Want it Now!

A MEMOIR OF LIFE ON THE SET OF

Willy Wonka
and The Chocolate Factory

Julie Dawn Cole
The Original Veruca Salt

WITH MICHAEL ESSLINGER

I Want it Now!

A Memoir of Life on the Set of Willy Wonka and the Chocolate Factory

By Julie Dawn Cole with Michael Esslinger

For information contact:

BearManor Media
P. O. Box 71426
Albany, GA 31708

bearmanormedia.com

First edition

ISBN: 1-59393-074-7

Original Book Design and Composition by John Reinhardt
Original Book Cover Design by Jim Zach

This book is dedicated
to the memory of my mum,
and the futures of Holly India,
and Barney.

Introductory Note

Who would have thought that after almost 40 years, people would still be interested in the kids from *Willy Wonka*? As wide-eyed, enthusiastic adolescents, we all happened to be at the right place at the right time to be part of something special. As Charlie, I have fond memories of my brief cinematic career. I couldn't have shared it with a better group of young professionals. However, Julie will always have a special place in my heart for her performance as Veruca Salt. I was awestruck when I heard her sing "I Want It Now"!

It was definitely the musical high point for the film.

As Willy Wonka said, and I concur, "A thing of beauty is a joy forever". I actually think he was describing Julie's performance.

With great affection,

Peter Ostrum
"Charlie Bucket"

Contents

Contents

Preface

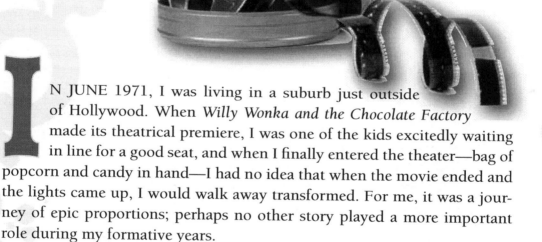

IN JUNE 1971, I was living in a suburb just outside of Hollywood. When *Willy Wonka and the Chocolate Factory* made its theatrical premiere, I was one of the kids excitedly waiting in line for a good seat, and when I finally entered the theater—bag of popcorn and candy in hand—I had no idea that when the movie ended and the lights came up, I would walk away transformed. For me, it was a journey of epic proportions; perhaps no other story played a more important role during my formative years.

In a very real sense, my life has been shaped by the world of cinema and in many ways, *Willy Wonka and the Chocolate Factory* was a prominent engineer of my own morals. Charlie Bucket, a quintessential compass of good character, embodied the enduring truth that making the right decision is often the hardest. Nevertheless, it was the abstract idea of Willy Wonka that touched my heart, as it has the hearts of many who've watched it. What made this film legendary was that audiences saw little parts of themselves in each of the characters. *Willy Wonka and the Chocolate Factory* is an archetypal flight of imagination—an adventure like no other.

Preface

Julie Dawn Cole, who played the nasty Veruca Salt in the movie, offers a rare glimpse behind the stage curtain, chronicling the journey that helped bring Roald Dahl's classic story to the screen. Julie's portrayal of the spoiled "material girl" is dead on, but when we began working together, I found that there is barely a trace of Veruca in her own life; her character rendering was in complete opposition to her own personality. Where did she find Veruca Salt? I can only conclude that it was her love of the theater and ability to tap into a difficult childhood that brought forth such a convincing portrayal.

Some of the most seasoned filmmakers of that era placed Julie in the same class as the young Judy Garland. Frawley Becker, who in his prolific career worked behind the camera with an iconic list of stars that included Spencer Tracy, Katharine Hepburn, Ann-Margaret, Peter O'Toole, Omar Sharif, Christopher Plummer, and Audrey Hepburn, once commented that "her amazing voice in *Willy Wonka* resonates in your ear long after the picture ends." Walter Scharf, another Hollywood veteran nominated for no less than ten Academy Awards, expressed a similar opinion of Julie's memorable performance. Perhaps the most satisfying compliment came from the movie's director. In a 2003 interview, when Mel Stuart was asked about his favorite memory of the film, he said simply that it was Julie's performance.

In the early 1970s, Hollywood's Sunset Boulevard was lined with stores that sold movie memorabilia and specialty books. I have long been an aficionado of these "on-location" and "the making of" books because they give the reader a peek into magic worlds in which characters and visual poems are engineered by human imagination. What was essentially a very practical process in terms of writing and production seemed to have magical elements that surfaced when projected on the screen.

A young boy with an unquenchable curiosity, I went to extreme measures to catch a glimpse of the process. At MGM, for example, several of the soundstages were closely adjacent to the public sidewalk on Washington Boulevard. A simple peek into one of these massive structures offered glimpses of both the exotic and the mundane. A grand sense of movement and excitement resonate from these sets; music, thunderous sound effects, and singing gave background to the noise of snapping hammers as sets were built and something extraordinary was created. These were the soundstages where *The Wizard of Oz* had been filmed, and though it was thirty years after the fact, I still expected to find a young Judy Garland sipping tea with her *Oz* co-stars between takes.

While one could argue that the words "magic" and "magical" are over-used in this book, it is indeed pure magic to get an inside look at such a legendary film directly from someone who participated in its creation. When the opportunity came to work with Julie and to learn more about one of my all-time favorite movies, I jumped at the chance.

In my professional career, I have interviewed a variety of people that represent a full spectrum of the human experience. From the first astronauts who walked on the moon to numerous men who served time on Alcatraz. However, I can safely state, bar none, Julie's memoir ranks as one of the most interesting human stories about a film that has inspired millions of people around the globe. She has seen the scale of life balanced in every direction, and I know that you are going to walk away seeing *Willy Wonka and the Chocolate Factory* and the person behind Veruca Salt in an even more enchanting light than before.

—Michael Esslinger

Introduction

"We begin with five Golden Tickets, like five lucky bolts of lightning, ready to strike, without notice, at any point on the map..."

LITTLE DID I KNOW that one of those lightning bolts was headed in my direction! This is the story of how I became Veruca Salt, and my memories of my early years and of life on the set of *Willy Wonka and the Chocolate Factory*. It is also about how Veruca became part of me and helped shape my future. To borrow loosely from Shakespeare's Hamlet, Veruca Salt thus became my native hue of resolution.

Magical? Oh, yes, it *was* magical. Looking back, it was charmed—even surreal in its way. It's unlikely that any of us child actors really understood the significance—or staying power, for that matter—the movie would have in the lives of others. We had no idea at all. It was special to us, yet all of us

were very young and just getting started in our careers. Most of us didn't have enough experience to know whether this was normal or something more. How naïve we all were, how innocent.

Today, it's a wondrous gift to see not just children but also their parents brighten with genuine enchantment as they talk about what *Willy Wonka and the Chocolate Factory* meant to them. Our producer, David Wolper, one of Hollywood's most successful and influential and also the recipient of countless Academy Awards, Emmys and Golden Globes, wrote in his memoir that despite producing landmark films and television shows, it is not until *Willy Wonka* is mentioned that deep *awe* strikes.

Willy Wonka has proven itself a favorite film of children around the world, and even after nearly four decades, it retains a powerful cultural resonance. Inspired by Roald Dahl's classic children's novel, the enduring film continues to enchant both young and old. For me, the movie holds many special memories. The vivid cinematic landscapes, the memories of youthful friendships, and the timeless story captured on film for future generations of children to enjoy—Dahl's magical world is an old friend with a charmed heritage.

I've long wondered what made our film a cultural phenomenon. Though I've never been able to put my finger on it exactly, and the recipe for its longevity still eludes me, I do at least know some of the ingredients. The world of filmmaking has evolved over the past few decades, and in many fantasy-themed films today, cinematic landscapes and even characters are very often computer-generated. It's common for actors to work in front of green screens and interact with phantom objects, leaving the crafting of the magical images to technological post-production wizards. Yet, in the case of *Willy Wonka and the Chocolate Factory*, the wonderment, the excitement, and the magic captured on screen was all genuine. For the most part, what the audience saw, was what we saw.

Though we were acting on soundstages, many of the visual aspects were real environments created with life-sized props, back projection and analog effects. Some of the early script versions didn't reveal the surprises we would encounter, and it was our genuine unscripted reactions that were captured on film. Despite having seen many of the sets in their unfinished forms during pre-production, nothing fully prepared us for the moment we finally emerged into the rainbow swirl of color and light that made up this imaginary place.

In the late 1990s, as the thirtieth anniversary of the film's release approached, I attended a couple of cast reunions. People traveled from all over to hear our stories, and pressed us to recall even the smallest details of the *Willy Wonka* production. They were also interested in our personal journeys, our lives after the movie—how the captivating world of *Willy Wonka and the Chocolate Factory* served as a launching pad for our futures.

Each of the *Wonka* kids explored different life paths following their signature roles. Peter Ostrum, cast as the lovable Charlie Bucket, gave up acting of his own accord, despite lucrative contract offers. Most of the others also eventually abandoned acting for other equally fulfilling and successful endeavors. But all of us remain forever bonded through those timeless on-screen characters, who, despite their exaggerated flaws, somehow continue to endear themselves to audiences.

Exploring my old boxes of *Wonka* memorabilia and reliving these treasured memories has been an extraordinary experience. It is a link to a very special part of my life and some early friendships that I have long treasured. Sadly, some of those friends have passed away: Jack Albertson (Grandpa Joe), Roy Kinnear (who played my ever-pleasing father and spoiled me both on- and offscreen), Nora "Dodo" Denney (Mrs. Teevee), Ursula Reit (Mrs. Gloop), Günther Meisner (Arthur Slugworth), Pat Coombs (my mother, Henrietta), David Battley (Mr. Turkentine, Charlie's quirky teacher), many of the original Oompa Loompas, and even Roald Dahl, the inventor and architect of this astonishing world. These wonderful people, along with so many other greats from the production side, continue to entertain us, and I will forever be connected to them and what we created together. My memories tie me to a place to which I still go in my dreams—a landscape that will always be a part of me. The happily-ever-after ending was, of course, a Hollywood fable, but the complex and mythical tale of goodness conquering greed is ageless and just as everlasting as a Gobstopper. The image has yet to fade.

"Ladies and Gentlemen, Boys and Girls . . . The Chocolate Room"

I REMEMBER HOW EXCITED all of us were the day we began shooting the Chocolate Room scene. While we had seen many of the sets being built on various soundstages, the mammoth Chocolate Room set had remained off-limits. Well, sort of. Okay, my first secret is out of the bag. A month before filming, I had traveled to the studio to record the "I Want It Now" musical track, and everyone asked me if I'd like a peek at set designer Harper Goff's not-quite-finished masterpiece. Director Mel Stuart had worked to isolate the child actors from this particular location during construction. He felt that by removing us from the technical elements of the production, our first reactions to seeing the Chocolate Factory would be unscripted and genuine, reflecting a real sense of purity and excitement. Mel was so pleased at being able to reveal his "surprise" that I was afraid to own up for fear of spoiling it for him. I decided to keep quiet—which I have, until now. But on the day we shot this particular scene, nothing prepared me for seeing it in its completed form.

We all stood on the far side of the massive façade steel door with its large button rivets and artful patches of rust, nervously waiting to catch our first glimpse of the set. Gene Wilder lightened the mood as we got into character

Gene Wilder in his signature role as the unforgettable Willy Wonka.

and awaited our cue. I was the lucky one; my character, Veruca, demanded to be first in line, so I would be the first to see it. We waited anxiously for what seemed to be forever. As the production crews put on the finishing touches and our youthful energy was becoming hard to contain, we finally heard Mel's bullhorn-blared signal: "Background...and...ACTION!"

As the colossal door began its slow, steady swing open, I peered around it as soon as there was enough space for my head. Once all of us were inside, we marveled at the majestic chocolate waterfall, the sweet and colorful vistas, candy forests, oversized mushrooms and gummy bears—they all seemed to be straight out of an enchanting storybook. The fairy-tale world imagined by Dahl and brought to life by Harper Goff was indeed "pure imagination." As we entered and began to savor our surroundings, it became clear that the Chocolate Room would also be one of the film's central characters. We were encouraged to explore without any specific direction, guided by the edible elements of the candy props.

Off-camera, I sought out this particular set, and often ate my lunch by the chocolate river whilst listening to the "Pure Imagination" musical track that played in the background.

Much as the door to the Chocolate Room was my entry into an astonishing cinematic world, *Willy Wonka and the Chocolate Factory* opened the curtain on the stage that was my life.

Above: *In Search of the Castaways*, with Hayley Mills, Maurice Chevalier and Keith Hamshere was a favorite movie from my youth. I loved this film as a child and Hayley Mills was my adventurous heroine who I aspired to emulate.

Right: Hayley on the set of *In Search of the Castaways*.

The Early Years

From early childhood, I've cherished a deep and passionate love for the cinema. I can still recall the excitement that gripped me when the theater lights finally dimmed and the silver screen magically transformed into an enchanted world—I was drawn right into the adventure.

My favorite film as a child was Walt Disney's epic, *In Search of the Castaways*, based on Jules Verne's novel, *Les Enfants du Capitaine Grant*. The theater lobby posters—brightly lit and proclaiming "A Thousand Thrills and Hayley Mills!"—captivated me. In this romantic nineteenth-century adventure, she was cast as Mary Grant, daughter of a shipwrecked sea captain. As the story unfolded, I felt as though Hayley and I were partners in the escapades that followed her discovery of a message in a bottle, which she believed came from her missing father. Together, we set out on a journey that took us across vast oceans, encountering earthquakes, floods, child-snatching raptors, and even a cannibal tribe along the way.

So vivid is this early memory that I can still hear Maurice Chevalier singing in his wonderful French accent, "Why cry about bad weather...Enjoy it...Each moment is a treasure...Enjoy it..." He whistled and sang as he cooked birds' eggs in a hollowed ombú tree trunk, where he sat gaily marooned after a torrential flood. The music, the adventure, and Hayley's hints of young romance swept me away. But when the lights came up and the screen went black, I slipped back into my loving but conflicted family, and the financial instability that always seemed to plague us. Unlike Hayley's character, Mary Grant, my message in a bottle was still lost at sea.

I was born in October 1957, in Guildford, a small and picturesque suburb of Surrey, England. Guildford is situated thirty miles southwest of London and has a past that extends far back into the mists of British history.

In the 1950s, Guildford was a bustling English town, where modern trends contrasted with historic cobbled streets. A castle, early 16th century dwellings, a lush green landscape, and an occasional riverboat accounted for much of the town's charm. While 1957 brought little change to Guildford's landscape, the larger world was fast entering the modern age. Russia had launched its Sputnik satellite. In Liverpool, two young musicians named John Lennon and Paul McCartney had just formed the Quarrymen, and British radio stations were airing the new sounds of rock and roll with Elvis Presley's chart-topping "All Shook Up" and "Jailhouse Rock." But all of this was worlds away from the realities of my modest upbringing. In many ways, my childhood most resembled the life of Charlie Bucket rather than Veruca Salt.

My family history is a bit sketchy, with a speck of scandal. Very little is known about my grandparents' lives; in fact, my mother, Patricia Williams, knew about her father only through the subtle hints my grandmother occasionally let slip. But those clues might be insights to the beginnings of my theatrical bloodline. Years ago, when tracing my family tree, I was stunned to find evidence (or at least a strong possibility) that my grandmother had married bigamously! Records reveal two marriages spaced ten years apart, and curiously enough, both reference her age as twenty-two. My grandmother used to hint about a trumpeter with whom she fell in love at about the time of my mother's birth in 1934. Whenever Jan Ralfini's Orchestra came up in conversation, or played on the radio, she would lean in and comment, with a wry smile: "You should really pay attention to them, you know."

One of the earliest photos of my sister Lynn (seen holding her doll) and me taken with our mother in January of 1958. Little did she know that our lives were barreling towards a waterfall.

I Want it Now!

Ralfini's Orchestra was a popular fixture in 1930s London. As a youth, Jan Ralfini and his father toured British cinemas, playing background music for silent films. Later, as "big band" music swept across Europe and America, Ralfini cashed in on the public's enthusiasm for big hall dances. Ralfini's band toured London halls, and his shows brimmed with popular orchestral hits and vaudevillian comedy routines that left the audiences roaring with laughter. The shows were routinely broadcast on local radio stations, and Ralfini was a favorite of those who could not afford the London night scene. Since his touring group comprised of only twelve players, the number of likely suspects as to my grandmother's Romeo were limited. But we were never to find out; she never revealed the identity of her lover, and my mother was left to dream and wonder.

The Early Years

My mother and my father, Peter Dennis Cole, both natives of Guildford, met as teenagers at a local speedway. At sixteen, she was love-struck by the young Peter Cole. He sported a cool bike, which impressed her, and he was impressed by her grace and elegance. Sparks quickly ignited, and they were engaged on my mother's seventeenth birthday and married less than two years later. In 1956, my sister Lynn was born; I followed seventeen months later. But for my mother, the happiness quickly faded, and their relationship became both isolating and torturous.

My memories of my father are sketchy and few. There were no kind words or loving gestures at home. In fact, I was incredibly frightened of him, and withered in the repressive environment he fostered in our home; his resentment towards us was palpable. Even at a young age, I was aware of the unhappy atmosphere, which often translated to violence towards my mother. I began to experience psychosomatic illnesses comprising of mystery aches and pains, a stomach cramps which didn't fit any medical diagnosis. The stony silences directed at my sister and I were equally painful. Despite this, my mother did her best to provide a good home, and was unfailingly compassionate and protective. Then, when I was six, our father left without fanfare or goodbye. He walked out on his three girls and never returned, an event that altered our lives forever.

A very rare photo of my mother and father (both very young) during happier times, and I expect close to when they were just married.

Above, right: A photo of me at the beach in Brighton when I was about four years old.

Above, left: My beautiful mother on her wedding day to my father Peter when she was only eighteen. My grandfather is seen at her side preparing to give her away.

Left: One of the only photos I have of all us together, not to mention our meager accommodations while on holiday at Hayling Island, a modest resort on the South Coast (my father is holding me and my sister is seated in the entry).

Below, right: Another young photo of me when I was about five years old taken at the beach.

Left: A very young photo me holding a jar of tadpoles at my great grandmother's cottage in Llangynidr, a small village community located in Wales. My great grandmother is on the far right with my grandmother and grandfather sitting next to her.

From this point on, we would always skate close to the brink of poverty. We lived in state-supported housing; there was no central heating, just a small coal fireplace in the main room downstairs. Our bedroom was so cold in the winter that ice would form on the inside of the window. Laundry was done by hand, and we had very few conveniences of any sort. Among my most distinct memories of this period is standing in the school lunch line, at the very back of the queue with the kids who qualified for free meals issued by the state. Despite this, my Mother taught us to hold our heads high and insisted that we behave better than everyone else so others would not stereotype us as low class. She was always dreaming of a better life for us and didn't want anybodies pity.

My mother was not just a hopeless dreamer. She made an earnest effort to fill our lives with wonderful experiences, including holiday celebrations—though admittedly, the trappings were modest. One such took place in 1968, during a family caravan vacation at Hampshire's Hayling Island Holiday Camp, a small seaside resort not far from our home. My mother had a close friend, Sean Casey, who was a costume designer for the National Theatre and other venues. Using fabric left over from a costume made for Richard Harris—either for his role as King Arthur in *Camelot* or possibly a stage production—Sean fashioned stylish capes for my sister and me. Mine was a flamboyant purple and hers, a dazzling red. My sister and I ran excitedly but stealthily through the amusement arcade in our smuggler-style

My mother seen decorating our home for the holidays around 1961. I'm not sure why she had such a serious look, but it's a photo of her I've always liked.

capes, carefully surveying each slot machine and hoping to strike it lucky by finding even a single coin. It was much more fun than it was profitable. Our biggest payout was finding enough to buy a hot dog, which we shared between three of us. At the end of the week the only food we had left, was the remnants of Kellogg's Frosted Flakes and half a jar of strawberry jam. This became breakfast, lunch and dinner on our final day before returning home to Guildford. But that holiday remains one of the happiest memories of my childhood.

I've sometimes wondered if my mother would have fought so hard to give us the few luxuries we had if she and my father had not divorced. It was my impression that she didn't want us to blame her for missing out on things. So, at an early age, my sister and I had ballet lessons. My sister soon gave them up and took up horseback riding instead, but I carried on. I was never destined to be a ballerina, but I liked the "pretend" aspect, and loved to dream.

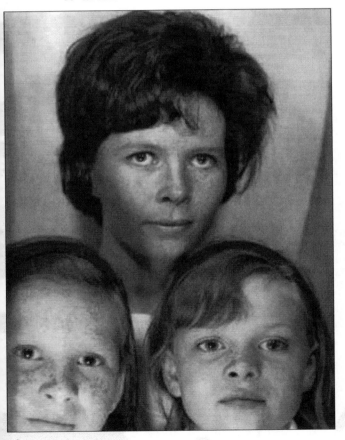

A single mother raising two daughters was almost unheard of in 1960s England, and I remember trying to find dignified ways to explain my father's absence. On at least one occasion, I told a friend that my father was a sailor and that was why he wasn't around. I was found out when my friend's mother discreetly commented to mine, "I gather your husband is a sailor, is he?" My ever-proud mother set the record straight with both of us, and that was the end of my fantasy-father embellishment.

I was around six when this photo was taken of my mother, sister and me in a photo booth while vacationing in Hayling Island.

Over time, we became accustomed to our way of life, and I enjoyed our close relationship. We did everything together. On Saturdays, we walked into town to do our shopping, going from store to store, searching for the cheapest prices for staples like eggs and milk. On Sundays, we baked all day. Music from the radio filled our home as we sang and danced to the hits of the era. I can still smell the pleasing aroma of bread fresh from the oven and hear us singing along to Brian Hyland's "She wore an itsy bitsy teeny weenie yellow polka dot bikini." I loved the fanciful melodies that sweetened the Sunday air. These are memories I still hold very dear today.

In addition to radio, we also had a small black-and-white television, which transported the three of us into the engrossing worlds of drama, suspense and science fiction. On Friday evenings, we rushed home, anxious not to miss *Burke's Law*, the gripping story of Los Angeles police chief of detectives Amos Burke, who just happened to be a multi-millionaire. Some of my other favorites included the

Above: A photo of me filled with laughter taken with my grandfather when I was eight years old. He passed away just a couple of years later in 1969.

Right: My sister Lynn's and my smuggler style capes that were designed and fashioned by Sean Casey.

fantastic worlds of Irwin Allen in *Voyage to the Bottom of the Sea* and the adventure series, *Land of the Giants*. The characters became my friends, imagined but also real in my mind's eye. *Lost in Space*, *Batman*, *Alfred Hitchcock Presents*, *Bewitched*, and even the comedic *Hogan's Heroes* all hold special places in my memory. They became what I looked forward to most in daily life, and I didn't want to miss any of their grand and sometimes dangerous adventures.

Our occasional weekend trips to the cinema were even more enchanting. I loved the Disney-era films with animal themes, like *Old Yeller* and *The Yearling*, and Cary Grant and Barbara Stanwyck were just two of my on-screen heroes. Now, decades later, the cinema still remains a favorite escape from my busy life.

Sean Casey (right), a costume designer for the National Theatre and his partner Robert Summers (left), relaxing in our family's backyard in Guildford. My mother had met Sean and became close friends during her time working in amateur theatre.

My sister and I somewhere on the South Coast wearing our matching blue polka dot dresses. I was around ten when this photo was taken.

My Grandmother was a vibrant, caring and high-energy spirit. Her adventurous nature and scandalous tales are among the things I miss most about her.

The Stage

ALTHOUGH I CAN'T put my finger on a single epiphany or profound theatrical experience, I know that I had an interest in acting from a very young age, which may have been instilled by my mother's love for the theater. She had performed in various amateur dramatics, including a local production of a play entitled *Love's a Luxury*, and her passion for the arts was a vital presence in our daily life.

I was inclined to be the joker of the family—I loved to entertain my sister and mother. During our more difficult times, when my mother was distraught over finances, laughter was the perfect diversion. My sister Lynn was more nurturing, more earnest; she took her homemaking role a little more seriously than I. But me—I was carefree and always a bit more light-hearted. I cherished the world of make-believe, for this is where real magic existed. No matter how low our spirits, I could always conjure up a smile with a little humor.

During my junior-school years, while attending the Bushy County Primary School in Merrow, about three miles outside of Guildford, I had a remarkable teacher, Kay Dudeney. At that time, drama was not part of the standard school curriculum; it had to be taken after school hours or in

My mother in the amateur stage production of *Love's a Luxury*. Her deeply rooted passion for the theatre undoubtedly had a profound influence on me during my formative years. I expect that it offered her a welcome escape from the daily pressures of being a single mother. In the late 1960s the theatre had become a family affair and both my sister and I took acting parts in some of the productions. Reflecting back on those memories, it was magical that the three of us were able to share in such an extraordinary experience together. I cherish these photos of my mother, as they capture the essence of her courageous and warmhearted spirit.

between classes. Kay was a wonderful educator, bursting with enthusiasm, who somehow managed to inspire her bunch of eight-year-olds. When she announced that the drama club was going to start, and that we would have to rehearse during the lunch hour, I couldn't wait to audition! The production was *Cinderella*, and how I wanted to play that part. Sadly, I didn't get it, but I did get the role of the Fairy Godmother—I was apparently the only one who owned a pair of ballet shoes with ribbons!

My most vivid memory of that first appearance onstage was waving my wand and announcing "Cinderella, you shall go to the ball…" What happened next was not exactly conventional. Rather than having stage fright before my performance, my attack came afterwards. Once offstage, I started to shake uncontrollably, so hard that someone wrapped me in a blanket, fearful that I was going to go into shock. But once the trembling passed, the only bug I had was for acting.

My sister Lynn and I performing in the local village hall as part of my mother's amateur theater group, the Merrow Players. It is the only photo of my sister and me performing together. I am seen on the far right kneeling and my sister is directly behind me in the dark dress. I was twelve and she was fourteen when this photo was taken.

I Want it Now!

My next amateur school production was a dream role. I was cast as Wendy in the enchanting tale, *Peter Pan*, by Scottish novelist and playwright Sir James Matthew Barrie. We performed in the school hall, which didn't have a proper stage. The flying rigs were made by our parents, who fabricated harnesses from simple cables thrown over the rafters. They also pulled the cables, manipulating us like puppets, and I pointed my toes as I swung through the air, flying to adventure. Still vivid in my memory is the marvelous moment when the children were asked if they believed in fairies, and the audience roared.

Me in a school production of the classic fairy tale of *Little Red Riding Hood*

The Stage

Right: Formal portrait as a student at the Bushy Hill County Primary School in Merrow. I was only eight years old.

Below: A cast photo from my very first junior school production of *Cinderella*. I didn't get the lead role as Cinderella, but I was cast as the Fairy God Mother, which I expect was mostly because I was the only one who owned a pair of formal ballet shoes (you can see me wearing them if you look very closely). It represents my very first public performance, as it was part of my afterschool drama class founded by my teacher Kay Dudeney. This experience at such a young age was very profound and helped chart my path into later becoming a professional actress. In 1997, I founded CenterStage, a Saturday morning theatre school for children in Surrey. Much of my inspiration came from those afterschool drama classes and as a result, Kay's legacy still lives on in my young pupils.

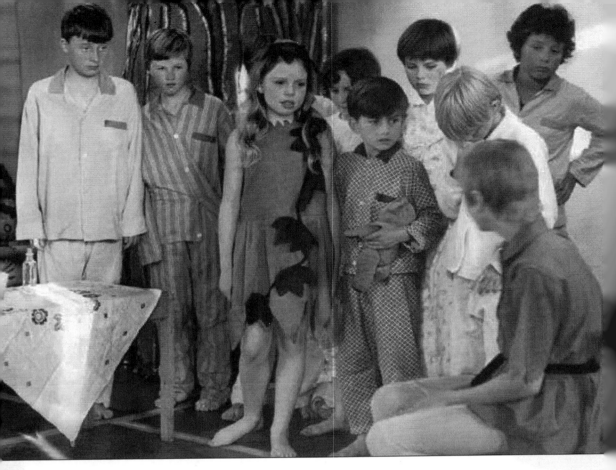

In 1968, I was cast as Wendy in our amateur school production of the classic *Peter Pan*. For me, landing this role was an absolute dream, and it didn't seem to matter that we didn't have a proper stage to perform on. The experience was profound on many different levels. It sowed the seeds for what has become a lifelong love for acting and the theater.

I was now thoroughly hooked, and not just by Captain Hook. *Peter Pan* provided the opportunity to perform, and the story's endearing characters moved the audience. This was a powerful realization.

I went on to act in several other school productions, including *Little Red Riding Hood*, the popular seventeenth-century folktale penned by Charles Perrault. For my farewell performance, I was cast as Yum-Yum, the love interest of Nanki-Poo, in Gilbert and Sullivan's grand opera, *The Mikado*. In retrospect, it was an extraordinary undertaking—a cast of ten-year-olds singing operatic four-part harmonies with romantic Japanese themes. These first steps set me on my path to the stage and planted seeds that would soon blossom.

In 1969, after passing an academic proficiency exam, I was faced with a wonderful dilemma. I had been extended an offer to attend the Guildford County Grammar School, a highly regarded local institution, but my teacher, Kay, encouraged my mother to let me pursue my interest in acting, and set up auditions for me at various stage schools. Kay was a keen observer, one able to see beyond the obvious. By this time, it was evident that acting was something I took very seriously, and Kay wanted me to cultivate that passion. It was an incredibly difficult decision for my mother—she knew that whatever path she chose would forever shape my future. But in the end, she took Kay's advice.

I auditioned for two stage schools; one was a day school and the other was boarding. The standard curriculum included a mix of academic work and formal theater studies. The schools all had professional agencies attached to them and if you were lucky, you could audition for roles in major productions. The schools said it was good experience for us, but they also acted as our agents and retained 25 percent for the service—a shockingly high (some might say immoral) portion. Particularly since, regardless of how much we generated for the institution, we were still required to pay the full (and expensive) school tuition.

I was accepted at both schools, but chose the Italia Conti Stage School in London as a day pupil, which was coincidentally, the creative platform for alumnus Anthony Newley, who co-wrote the musical numbers in *Willy Wonka and the Chocolate Factory*. Classes in drama, tap dancing, ballet, singing, and jazz were part of our daily academics. During our studies, the school's agents were busy arranging auditions, which took place both on and off campus. It was an intense schedule for an eleven-year-old.

Every day, I traveled two-and-a-half hours each way to London by bus and train. During these journeys, I read the classics, and through them, was introduced to many make-believe worlds. John Wyndham's novels— *The Day of the Triffids*, *The Kraken Wakes* and *The Midwich Cuckoos*—were among my absolute favorites. I even read some of the darker novels by Dennis Wheatley, which gripped my attention throughout the journey.

My first professional engagement came in 1969, two months after joining Italia Conti, when I was cast as Liza, the housemaid in *Peter Pan*. In 1904, Barrie's *Peter Pan* made its debut as a children's Christmas play in London, and quickly became an English Christmas tradition. I so loved this

I Want it Now!

Photos from my school production of Gilbert and Sullivan's grand opera, *The Mikado*. At only ten, I was cast as Yum-Yum and I loved performing the operatic Japanese themed romantic harmonies.

Hayley Mills during the 1969 London production of *Peter Pan*. Working together with Hayley during this production was dreamlike after having been such an adoring fan. She was a wonderful mentor and the experience has remained one of my most enchanting memories from my early years of acting.

enchanting fairytale, particularly with its memories of my amateur school production, and being cast in the London show as my first professional role, I felt as though I'd been sprinkled by fairy dust myself.

Rehearsals were held at the London Welsh Association's Rugby Club headquarters, and since I had only a few speaking parts, I was able to study the other actors and learn from the professional theater masters who developed the production. My first day at rehearsals also brought my first brush with stardom. As I entered the rehearsal hall, the young girl in front of me held the door open for me. At first, I didn't pay much attention, but I suddenly realized who the girl was: Hayley Mills, my favorite actress from *In Search of the Castaways*. She gave me a warm smile, and then, expecting me to reach out and grab the door, she let it go and continued into the building. I simply stood in awe as the door swung closed. Then, after regaining my composure, I finally entered. Hayley Mills had literally opened the door to my first professional stage role.

Peter Pan opened at the New Victoria Theatre in December 1969. The effervescent Mills appeared in the title role; also in the cast was Bill Travers as Captain Hook. Travers was an established actor with a prolific film and television career, best known for his roles in *Born Free* with Virginia McKenna and *Rawhide* with Clint Eastwood. He was a wonderful man and I have fond memories of working with him.

The costumes and stage imagery remain as bright as Kodachrome snap-shots in my mind. Even some of my lines are still as clear as though I had learned them yesterday. My first scene was set in the Darling family nursery, where Wendy, John and Michael were tucked in bed asleep; their parents had left Nana, the family dog, to serve as their guardian, and Liza the house-maid, to watch over them. While trying to catch his mischievous shadow, Peter Pan, along with his fairy, Tinker Bell, entered the nursery. After a dis-tressing and fruitless attempt to get his shadow to stick, he was comforted by Wendy. The other children awoke and Peter offered to teach them to fly under the London starlight. Liza entered the nursery to investigate the cause of Nana the dog's barking. The children pretended to be asleep as I was dragged onstage by the enormous Saint Bernard dog which was actually a grown man in a furry costume. My character was in a bad temper because of Nana's ceaseless barking and because she had been disturbed while mix-ing Christmas puddings in the kitchen. My first professional lines were, "There, you suspicious dog, they're perfectly safe, aren't they? Every one of the little angels is sound asleep in bed. No more of it, Nana."

We doubled up on parts, and I remember the excitement of dressing up as wolves and Indians and other characters. One humorous event occurred during the second act. The scene opened with a mother mermaid and a baby mermaid (me) sitting on a rock. To simulate the ocean's waves, a gauze cloth was painted below the rocks to create the illusion of water. At the top of the scene, mother and baby mermaid were to take flight when Peter came with his lost boys, entering the "water" with a splash and sliding down a big plank. But in order to slide gracefully across the stage, you had to have momentum. On this particular performance, mommy mermaid didn't achieve it, and when she was about halfway down, the plank tipped up as I followed. As a result, I lost my own momentum and had to crawl com-mando-style on my elbows, dragging my mermaid tail, across the massive New Victoria Theatre's stage. This drew much laughter from the audience. In another scene, in which I played one of the wolves after a quick change in my dressing room three flights up, I rushed onstage at the last minute. Putting on my wolf mask, I inadvertently pulled it down so far that the eye holes were at my cheeks. I couldn't see anything, and stumbled around the stage crashing into the various props and scenery.

For Christmas, Hayley Mills gave me my first bottle of perfume, Mary Quant, which was quite a thrill. But the memory that stands out for me was the first and only time in my life I have ever missed a performance. On Christmas Eve, I came down with the flu, and regardless of how much I pleaded with my mother to let me travel to London, she refused. So I was sick *and* furious!

Under London's bright starlight, the enchanting story of Peter Pan thrilled audiences for six weeks. It was a charmed experience for me, and continues to hold a very special place in my heart.

My official publicity photo from Barbra Speake Stage School (1970).

Crossroads

THE UNFORGETTABLE STORY of *Charlie and Chocolate Factory* was written by Roald Dahl and published in 1964. Dahl, one of the most loved children's book authors of the twentieth century, was devoted to chocolate; he compared the classic chocolate treats invented during the 1930s to the great works of Bach and Mozart. By the time *Charlie and the Chocolate Factory* was published, Dahl was already well known for his dark and adventurous children's tales: *The Gremlins*, originally published by Walt Disney in 1943, and *James and the Giant Peach* (1961), which came to be considered a contemporary classic. But the touching story of *Charlie and the Chocolate Factory* quickly amassed its own dedicated following around the globe.

As was later acknowledged by the film's director, Mel Stuart, the idea to transform Dahl's masterpiece from print to film actually came from his ten-year-old daughter, Madeline. Her love for Dahl's eccentric and moralistic tale ultimately inspired her father to option the motion picture rights. Early on, the story's complex elements sparked a debate about making it as an animated feature, but eventually, discussions always came back to a traditional format.

Madeline's timing couldn't have been more perfect. Mel finished reading the book and pitched the idea to his colleague, David L. Wolper (principal of Wolper Productions) at the same time that Quaker Oats was looking for marketing opportunities for their new confectionary creations. Quaker Oats had a well-established and successful working relationship with Wolper and his team, and Quaker's ad agent, Ken Mason, was looking for a vehicle to promote a new candy bar under development. These concepts converged and lightning struck: The creation of *Willy Wonka and the Chocolate Factory* was set in motion.

Charlie and the Chocolate Factory was optioned for $200,000, which, even by today's standards, was a considerable sum, but the agreement came with a number of conditions. One essential component was that Dahl himself would write the screenplay. In the end, another brilliant writer, David Seltzer, was hired to augment the story with dramatic elements not in the original book. Wolper negotiated the title change to *Willy Wonka and the Chocolate Factory* to help brand Quaker's new chocolate bar, and also to provide a unique name mark for the production. But, halfway around the world, I was oblivious to all these goings-on.

During the production of *Peter Pan*, I developed close friendships with a few other child actors who were attending the Barbara Speake Stage School in East Acton. While I enjoyed the artistic atmosphere at Italia Conti, it became more and more clear that Speake's school held greater promise for me academically, and in January 1970, I transferred there. Located in the heart of a tough West London neighborhood, the school offered places not only to those with pedigree lineages but also to kids from working-class families. Barbara Speake had a lively artistic atmosphere, and despite its youthful enrollment, many of the students were seasoned performers. The morning assembly had a formality that reflected a working studio environment rather than an academic institution, with a roll call closely akin to a studio casting call. As our names were announced, so were our professional acting assignments, along with call times and venues. The school's faculty also molded our styles and personas. Individuality was frowned upon, and the female students followed a popular yet conservative look; once, when I decided to cut my hair a little shorter, I was called in and reprimanded for veering from these standards.

One of my first publicity photographs taken during the same period as *Willy Wonka*. This particular photo was taken at Barbara Speakes's home in London (1970).

The agency was run by June Collins. June—level-headed, unemotional, shrewd in her approach, detached, and with a meticulous demeanor—was the polar opposite of Barbara Speake, who was much more flamboyant and animated with her students. June's son was Genesis front-man Phil Collins, with whom I had a music lesson at one point; other Genesis band members were frequently seen at our school. Peter Gabriel's wife was my English teacher for a time, and her sister, also a teacher, became one of my favorites. Jack Wild, best known for his role as the teenage Artful Dodger in *Oliver*, and later as Jimmy in the cult favorite, *H.R. Pufnstuf*, frequently stopped by to see June, who continued as his agent following his graduation. The stage school was a beehive of developing talent, and lineups for casting agents, readings, and auditions were part of the daily ritual for students.

Casting for *Willy Wonka and the Chocolate Factory* began in January 1970. Wolper Productions hired Mary Selway for the London casting, which included auditioning young actresses for the role of Veruca Salt. For this particular audition, all of the girls in the preteen and early-teen age groups were brought into the school hall and lined up. The casting agents quickly scanned the group, pacing the line and pointing to each girl: "You...you, no...no...no, okay, you...," and so on. The first round of questions was simple: "What's your name? How old are you? Where do you come from?" and then it was back to class as normal.

The follow-up shortlist was a little more intense, with more questions and dialog. Finally, I was recalled to meet the director Mel Stuart and producer Stan Margulies. Up to this point, I wasn't familiar with any of Dahl's work, so when I was told that I had been called for the next round, I was instructed by June to read the book. With the assistance of our school's bus driver, we rushed around trying to find a copy of *Charlie and the Chocolate Factory*. We searched numerous bookstores before finally locating one in Hammersmith. I savored Dahl's chocolate opus on the train ride back to Guildford, and when I got home, secluded myself with the tale. And so began my acquaintance with Veruca Salt. Transfixed by her character, I thought how wonderful it would be to have a role in this production. I recall reading the Chocolate Room scene and thinking that I'd love to see this fantastical place. I also remember wondering how on earth the filmmakers were going to create it.

The final audition took place in a suite at the Kensington Hilton, and when my mother and I arrived in London by train, she decided that in order to make a proper entrance, we had to arrive in a black London taxicab. This notion was incredibly extravagant, but I have to admit that it added to my excitement.

Mel intimidated me from the moment I entered the suite. He had a scary presence, barking orders rather than speaking, and gave the impression that he made no allowances for anyone, especially children. Since no script existed at this stage, I was asked to read an extract from the book. I read a passage from "Veruca in the Nut Room," in which she demands that her father get her one of Wonka's specially trained squirrels. As her father gently tries

A candid photo of Jack Wild on the set of the Columbia Pictures classic motion picture Oliver! Nominated for twelve Academy Awards with the tagline "More of a Masterpiece than a Musical!" Oliver! won the Oscar for Best Picture and dominated the award categories next to films like *Chitty Chitty Bang Bang, 2001: A Space Odyssey, Bullitt, Funny Girl,* and *The Subject was Roses* to name only a few. Jack was nominated for Best Actor in a Supporting Role for his unforgettable performance as the Artful Dodger, but ironically lost to our own Jack Albertson for his role in *The Subject* was Roses, opposite Patricia Neal (Roald Dahl's wife—who also received a nomination for Best Actress in a Leading Role). Jack and I shared June Collins as our agent, and she continued in this role even after he graduated from Barbara Speake. Jack had reprised the role of the Artful Dodger which had been originally (and again ironically) played by Anthony Newley (the musical co-scribe for *Willy Wonka*) in the 1948 David Lean production, which had also been nominated for Best British Picture. Sadly, Jack died from cancer in 2006 at only fifty-three.

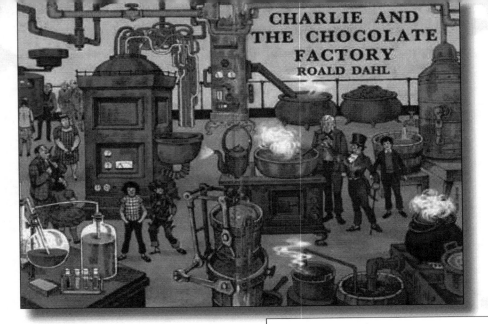

This book remains one of my greatest keepsakes from the production. It is my original copy of *Charlie and the Chocolate Factory* that I read from for my audition with Mel Stuart and Stan Margulies in London. I savored every page of this book and carried it with me during filming. My fellow actors each inscribed a special note next to their own character illustration, and my mother also wrote a special good luck message. It remains a treasured possession which I will never part with.

To My darling Julie.
Wishing you all the luck in the world dear,
with all my love
Mummy xxx

Dein nimmersatter Augustus
Michael Bölner

Then very slowly, with a slow and marvellous grin spreading all over his face, Grandpa Joe lifted his head and looked straight at Charlie. The colour was rushing to his cheeks, and his eyes were wide open, shining with joy, and in the centre of each eye, right in the very centre, in the black pupil, a little spark of wild excitement was slowly dancing. Then the old man took a deep breath, and suddenly, with no warning whatsoever, an explosion seemed to take place inside him. He threw up his arms and yelled "*Yippeeeeeeee!*" And at the same time, his long bony body rose up out of the bed and his bowl of soup went flying into the face of Grandma Josephine, and in one fantastic leap, this old fellow of ninety-six and a half, who hadn't been out of bed these last twenty years, jumped on to the floor and started doing a dance of victory in his pyjamas.

"*Yippeeeeeeeee!*" he shouted. "Three cheers for Charlie! Hip, hip, hooray!"

At this point, the door opened, and Mr. Bucket walked into the room. He was cold and tired, and he looked it. All day long, he had been shovelling snow in the streets.

"*Cripes!*" he cried. "What's going on in here?"

It didn't take them long to tell him what had happened.

"I don't believe it!" he said. "It's not possible."

"Show him the ticket, Charlie!" shouted Grandpa Joe, who was still dancing around the floor like a dervish in his

46

to discourage this notion, she begins listing her family pets while becoming more passionate in her demands. As I read the passage, Mel became animated, and his voice rose as he goaded me: "Be nasty…be mean…more, more…meaner, meaner…." Due to my mother's exceptional parenting, I'm proud to say that Veruca's nasty nature didn't come easy to me, and it was only through enormous effort that I was able to manage what proved to be a winning performance in Mel's eyes. When it came to the singing audition, I gave a lively rendition of *Happy Birthday*.

Mel began quizzing me about my acting experience, which caught me off guard; aside from *Peter Pan*, I had not been in any other productions. I was a complete beginner. I decided to fib, embellishing my résumé with fellow classmates' roles. I remember being completely unafraid of getting caught. I thought that if Mel found out, he would be impressed that I had the nerve to lie—that this very Veruca Salt–like behavior would weigh 'in' my favor rather than against me. (My embellishments came back to haunt me. When Paramount Pictures later distributed press kits, my bio included the motion picture *Melody*, costarring with Jack Wild. Although we had the same agent, my role was limited to one-day's work as a supporting artist). Following the audition, Stan and Mel thanked me and said they would contact my agent if they needed further information. Then, it was back on the train, and I returned to the classroom.

Just hours later, as I sat at my desk, June Collins entered the classroom and announced that I would be absent during the next term, since I would be going away to appear in very big movie! My classmates cheered, and their applause was grand. Jubilant, I couldn't wait to share the news with my mother and sister, but in this era of pre-mobile phones that moment would have to wait until I got home from school.

Next to the hotel where I auditioned for Mel and Stan is Kensington Gardens, where Peter Pan lived among the fairies. Perhaps Tinker Bell had sprinkled a little fairy dust on me, because on the train ride home, I was flying. I still have the copy of *Charlie and the Chocolate Factory* that I read from that day, and I cherish it—its pages retain the magic of the experience.

Initially, I had very little to help me prepare me for the role of Veruca. Roald Dahl was still working on the screenplay, and I was left to study the book, which I did, diligently. During this process, Mel sent Mary Selway's agency a demo LP with Anthony Newley singing each number and Leslie Bricusse on piano. The letter that accompanied it read:

> Dear Ms. Speake,
> Mel Stuart has asked us to send you the enclosed song from Charlie, along with the words. Would you please see that this song gets over to my dear darling Veruca, Julie Dawn.
>   Sincerely,
>   Assistant to Mary Selway

I played the album over and over, noting every nuance of my musical number. I also rehearsed with my singing teacher, Mrs. Le Touzel, who played "I Want It Now" on the school's organ. I studied the music so intently that even lyrics cut from the film are still fresh in my mind—one of the refrains that didn't make the final cut went:

> I want a ride in a fine crystal carriage; I want each day to be spring.
> And when the time comes to talk about marriage, I want a king.
> I want the stars, up in the heavens.
> Venus and Saturn all set in a pattern, can't wait to wear that on my brow.
> Don't care how . . .
> I Want it Now!

After studying the music, I was asked to meet with and sing for musical director Walter Scharf. Walter, another heavy in the film industry, had already amassed an impressive résumé. An accomplished composer in his own right, he had worked with everyone from Shirley Temple to Jerry Lewis. In his lifetime, he would be nominated for no less than ten Academy Awards. One of those was for *Willy and Wonka and the Chocolate Factory*, and was shared with Newley and Bricusse.

We met at the Dorchester Hotel on Park Lane, in a private room just off the bar. In another strange coincidence, the Dorchester had been a popular venue for Jan Ralfini and his orchestra, as well as the famed trumpeter Jack Jackson. While Walter sat at a vintage grand piano and adeptly played the fanciful melody to "I Want It Now," I sang my heart out, investing each lyric with Veruca's demanding passion. After just a couple of runs through the

I Want it Now!

Anthony Newley, British actor, singer and composer who wrote all of the musical elements for *Willy Wonka* with writing partner Leslie Bricusse. The demo recordings of all the compositions were recorded by Bricusse on piano and Newley on vocals. The early arrangements were jazz flavored and aside from the basic melody, nearly all of the pieces had syncopated rhythm styles paired with Newley's trademark vibratos. Prior to the production, all of us were provided with copies of these recordings for study, and Newley's distinctive voice could be heard echoing through our house for hours on end. But the final orchestral arrangements scarcely resemble the original lounge style jazz pieces. I still own the original recordings of Newley and they are all nostalgic reminders of the early beginnings of *Willy Wonka*.

music, Walter smiled and commented: "Yeah...I think you can do it." Thus was the decision made that I would sing the song in the film myself.

My next meeting was with costume designer Helen Colvig to begin work on my wardrobe. Helen was also a prominent figure in costume design; her very first credit was working with Alfred Hitchcock on *Psycho*. Helen showed me the concept sketches, and then I was measured for my dress. Following this, we were whisked off to Harrods and the Scotch House in Knightsbridge, London, to search for the kilt, yellow sweater, and shoes I was to wear in the factory scene in which my Golden Ticket is found. The sweater was itchy, but the shopping experience was marvelous.

Though I still hadn't seen the script, the character was beginning to gel, and the production schedule was now set. June Collins negotiated my contract, and all of the child actors received the same compensation, £60 per filming week. Twenty-five percent went to the school's agency (and I was still responsible for my academic fees). Even in those days, that was considered low on the wage scale for a production of this type. For example, in 1939, Jerry Maren was paid a salary of $50 per week for a supporting role in *The Wizard of Oz*; he was a member of the Lollipop Guild who welcomed Dorothy to Munchkinland (he was the one in green). But that really didn't matter. I was thrilled to be a part of it, and any amount was a welcome enhancement to our family's exceedingly modest income. Just to give a comparison, my mother's wage at this time was around £15 per week.

Selway Baker Ltd.

Casting Consultants

c/o Mediarts
39 Charing Cross Road,
London, W.C.2.

23rd July, 1970.

Miss Barbara Speake,
Barbara Speake Agency,
East Acton Lane,
London, W.3.

Dear Miss Speake,

JULIE DAWN
"CHARLIE AND THE CHOCOLATE FACTORY"

Mel Stuart has asked us to send you the enclosed song from
"Charlie.." with the words "would you please see that this song
gets over to my dear, darling Veruca - Julie Dawn" (!)

Yours sincerely,

ASSISTANT TO
MARY SELWAY

EVENING NEWS, Monday, July 27, 1970

ANTHONY NEWLEY and
Leslie Bricusse are writing
their first original score for a
film, Charlie and the Chocolate
Factory.

Directors: *Mary Selway*, *Beaty Baker*, *Miriam Brickman*, *J.D. Nightingirl*.

Munich

IN LATE AUGUST, I made my first trip to Munich, Germany, to visit the Bavarian Film Studios, where the massive sets were under construction, and also to record the guide track for the "I Want It Now" musical number.

Because the film's budget was modest—$2.9 million—Wolper Productions abandoned the idea of filming in Hollywood and looked for less expensive locations that would be unrecognizable to the audience. This was important because, to achieve a timeless quality and make the movie relevant for generations of audiences, the location needed unfamiliar architecture and cultural landmarks. David Wolper and Harper Goff embarked on a rigorous scouting expedition, visiting sites as various as a bankrupt chocolate factory in Spain and a beer factory, where they considered using its huge vats for the chocolate factory. But in every case, the locations didn't feel right for the essence of Dahl's masterpiece. Finally, after a string of disappointing visits, the team found the perfect location, one that offered the mammoth soundstages needed to accommodate the chocolate factory sets, as well as the technical capacity to fulfill the filmmakers' grand vision.

I Want it Now!

The studio was in the "film city" of Geiselgasteig, Bavarian Film Studio's headquarters. Alfred Hitchcock's first movie, *The Pleasure Garden*, had been filmed at Bavaria, and other classics had been shot on many of the same stages as *Willy Wonka*. These included scenes from Robert Wise's directorial epic, *The Sound of Music*, with Julie Andrews; John Sturges' *The Great Escape*, with Steve McQueen; Stanley Kubrick's *Paths of Glory*, with Kirk Douglas; and later, Bob Fosse's *Cabaret*, with Liza Minnelli and Joel Grey, to name but a few.

On August 24, 1970, nervous and excited, I stood clutching my teddy bear in the terminal of London's Heathrow Airport and met Sue Breen who I would spend the next three months with, for the first time. Sue was to be my chaperone as well as my tutor for the duration of the production. She was probably only in her late 20s, but in my eyes, seemed much older. Looking back on it now as a mother myself, I cannot imagine sending my child away with a stranger to a foreign country. The difficulties for both my mother and I remain something that we have never discussed to this day.

I kissed my mother and sister goodbye, promising to write home as often as I could, to share my adventures with them. I was sad to leave them behind, and felt guilty about embarking on such an exciting adventure without them. I had never been away from home before. I would be eating in exotic restaurants (or at least, exotic to me) and staying in nice hotels while they remained in our small, two-bedroom home in Guildford.

Though the flight from London to Munich was only two hours, the first thing I did was to write a letter to my mother. I had only been on a plane once before, to Jersey in the Channel Islands, and this international flight was very different. For one thing, food was served. In my letter, I described my culinary adventure:

There is slice of egg and cucumber, and tomatoes; a big slice of ham, the biggest you've ever seen; and an even bigger slice of turkey. This is all on top of a slice of brown bread and butter. There is also a tiny Danish pastry for pud [dessert]; in a tiny bag were salt and pepper pots, a sachet of mustard, some Marvel [a brand of powdered milk] and sugar. I drank the tea without sugar so that Lynn could have it [the sugar], and nearly poisoned myself.

HOTEL PALACE MÜNCHEN

Dear Mummy and Lyn,

I have arrived safely (as you probably know otherwise I wouldn't be writing this... I expect you are dying to know what it was like so I'll start right from the beginning. The plane was a Boeing Super 11 aeroplane. The plane was so big that we couldn't get seats near the window. We were about an hour late, we couldn't see the ground. I think I must have swallowed about 50 times before my ears stopped popping. He was brought round on trays with sort of compartment things in them...

...Lyn could have it and nearly poisoned myself.) We were flying at 2,800 ft and 500 to 800 miles per hour. We passed over Dover and Stuttgart... It was so sunny above the clouds that lots of people were wearing sunglasses, but they weren't just being nutty. The german word I saw was München. When we got off the plane it was raining (Naturally.) There was a blue bus waiting for us (like the one we will be having.) When we got to the customs a man in a green uniform went out saying in German so we said "English excuse" and we said so. When we first got into the building, we heard them announcing something about us on the intercom. All I heard was go to the Lufthansa information desk. Anyway we went there and the man said somebody was just coming to collect us. 2 secs later he came. I think he was the unit manager. He gave us our boarding expenses and an envelope with loads of other papers in it. He told us that we could go to Summer Party on Wednesday. I think his given Sue the tickets or whatever else we need for it. It should be fun because the people here are much more fun than the Northerns. These are really...

HOTEL PALACE MÜNCHEN

He took us to the hotel in his car. It's a grey saloon and terribly comfortable. The seats are covered in material like felt but it's super. When you sit on them its just like sitting on foam rubber. The hotel is lovely, its got big chandeliers in the foyer and lovely thick carpets. We are in a double room. It's got a bathroom going it which is lovely. The beds have got these big sort of eiderdown things on them instead of blankets and the pillows are square. I have just been to wash my face and I pressed the tap that had hot red knob on it. I started washing and thought funny the water's cold. Anyway I ran it for a while and it still didn't get warm. Then I turned on the other tap with a blue knob and Lo and Behold hot water. Trust me to do something stupid. That reminds me when we were driving along I saw the speed limit sign which said 80. Gosh they must limit it thought but then of course silly me had forgotten it was 80 kilometres per hour not in miles. Oh yes and bill name... the journey on the plane... he was wrong the journey on the plane was 1 hour 30 mins and half an hour from the airport to the hotel. There's supposed to be a swimming pool in the hotel somewhere. Sue said I'll find that later. Anyway whatever money is left after that the hotel bill is paid will divide between us 500 marks for both us and breakfast. I hate bed and breakfast for the rest of the day. The studios will probably do us lunch. We've got about another £50 for the rest of our food and doctors between us. The film company gave us a list of the rest of the foreign restaurants with the adresses. They also gave us a list of the rest of the cast and where they are staying. David Bartley is the only one in this hotel. So far Charlie and I are the only kids here apart from the families of the actors and so on. I'd better stop now because I'm going to have a bath, all my love

Julie

P.S. Give my love to Carol Chappy Pauline and Sandy
I'll write the rest as soon as I can.

I Want it Now!

When we finally arrived, we were taken straight to the very modern Hotel Palace Munchen, a stylish six-story, five-star hotel close to the River Isar and the English Garden. In two letters written a day apart, I described the hotel and included some other interesting details.

August 26, 1970

The hotel is lovely; it's got big chandeliers in the foyer and lovely carpets. We are in a double room. It's got a bathroom adjoining which is lovely. The beds have got those eiderdown things on them instead of blankets and the pillows are square. I have just been in to wash my face and I pressed the tap that had a red knob on it. I started washing and thought, funny, the water's cold. Anyway, I ran it for a while and it still didn't get warm. Then I turned on the other tap with the blue knob and lo and behold, hot water!

Sue said that whatever money is left after the hotel bill is paid we'll divide between us. It's about five hundred marks for both of us per week. That's bed and breakie [breakfast]. The studio will probably do us lunch. We've got about another sixty pounds for the rest of our food and extras between us. The film company gave us a list of foreign restaurants with the addresses. They also gave us a list of the cast and where they are staying. So far Charlie (Peter Ostrum) and I are the only kids here, apart from the family of the actors and so on. I'd better stop now because I'm going to have a bath.

August 27, 1970

I'm still enjoying it all but I want to come home. I had a horrible sleep because the pillow thing that's like an eiderdown kept falling off. My feet were sticking out of the bottom all night, the traffic was roaring past the bedroom and it was boiling hot.

During my first evening at the hotel, Sue and I met with British actor David Battley, who was cast as Charlie's quirky teacher, Mr. Turkentine. Battley was preparing for his classroom scenes, which were scheduled to begin filming on August 31. The three of us adjourned to the Palace's restaurant for a quiet dinner, and together, shared a strange experience. During our polite dinner conversation, he asked, "Where do you come from?" and

HOTEL PALACE MÜNCHEN

Dear Mummy, Papa, Nana + Carol,

...to tell everything it all but I want to come home. I'll tell everything I've done since Tuesday. Can you know what happened then, I had a horrible sleep, because the pillow thing, that like an eiderdown, that's one... falling... the coffee was roaring past the bedroom bottom all night, the coffee was roaring past the bedroom and it was looking, but life went into Munich babies and, tea (sorry I'm getting muddled up with babies and tea (sorry I'm in Munich) A studio car...

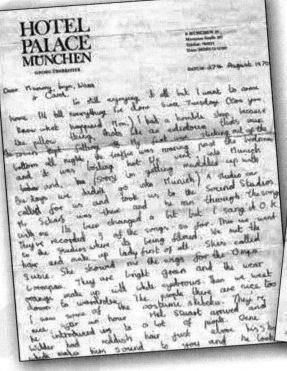

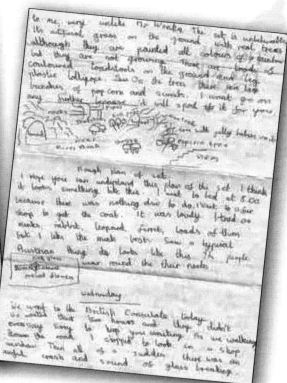

Wednesday

We went to the British Consulate today...

...some Sauerkraut. That's not your spell it I know...

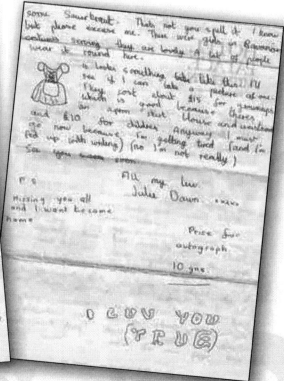

All my love,
Julie Dawn xxxx

P.S.
Missing you all
and I want to come
home

Price for
autograph
10 gns

I LUV YOU
(TRUE)

as I drew breath to answer, he blurted out "Guildford." We were all completely spooked. I asked him how he knew, and all he could say was that he sensed that was what I was going to say. It was one of those odd moments that has stayed with me for decades.

On August 26, I went to the music studio where all of the songs were being recorded. I wrote to my mother describing my first experiences of the session:

> *A studio car called for us and took us to the sound studio. Mr. Scharf was there and he ran through the song with me. It's been changed a bit, but I sang it okay. They've recorded three of the songs so far. Then we went to the studio where it is being filmed.*

The recording studio was situated in the city center. The orchestra had been in session, recording the musical score. This was my first time in a professional studio, so Walter Scharf gave me a quick tour of the facilities; then I

Jack and Peter recording their vocals for the "I've Got a Golden Ticket" musical track along with the production's Musical Supervisor Walter Scharf. I recorded my track in similar fashion with Walter by my side. Walter would share an Academy Award nomination alongside Bricusse and Newley for their work on *Willy Wonka*.

was handed a pair of headphones and directed to a microphone placed in the center of the large soundproof room. The experience was extraordinary! The music of the grand orchestra was piped into the headphones as I stood in a completely empty space. Under Scharf's direction, I recorded several guide track versions of "I Want It Now," which would be used for the final orchestral scoring. I then returned days later to record a semifinal version for rehearsals.

After this was done, I made my very first trip to the soundstages at Bavarian Film Studios. It was one of the most enchanting experiences to set eyes on the amazing and imaginary (and still unfinished) sets designed by Harper Goff. The scale was majestic, and Goff's imagination blossomed from the seeds planted by Dahl's prose. Goff had worked with Walt Disney and was one of the creative geniuses behind the epic *20,000 Leagues Under the Sea* (1954) and also *Fantastic Voyage* (1966). His designs were inventive,

Director Mel Stuart gave credit to Harper Goff for much of the film's success (seen here over-looking a scale model of the Chocolate Room set) resulting from his imaginative and colorful renderings of Dahl's story. Goff was one of Hollywood's top craftsmen of the age. The Academy Award winning creative genius behind Walt Disney's *20,000 Leagues Under the Sea* and the *Fantastic Voyage*, Goff used many of the original book illustrations to create the fantastical sets of *Willy Wonka*. Goff was also responsible for many of the early theme concepts of Disney's proposed "Mickey Mouse Park" which later became Disneyland.

colorful, and absolutely magical. Though still under construction, the sets looked just as fabulous in reality as they eventually did on film. My peek into the Chocolate Room gave me a glimpse of its enormous scale. Excerpts from my August 27 letter illuminate my excitement:

> *I went to the studios and met the hair and makeup lady, Susi [Krause] first of all; she showed me the wigs for the Oompa Loompas. They're bright green and they wear orange makeup with white eyebrows. Then we went to wardrobe, the people there are nice too, and I saw some of the costume sketches. After an hour, Mel Stuart arrived and he introduced us to a lot of people. Gene Wilder has reddish hair, just above his shoulders, which makes him sound to you, and he looks to me very unlike Mr. Wonka. The set is unbelievable, it has artificial grass on the ground with real trees, although they're painted all of the colors of the rainbow, but they are not growing. There are loads of colored toadstools on the ground, and big plastic lollipops. On the trees there are bunches of popcorn and sweets. I won't go any further because it will spoil it for you . . .*

It was during this first trip that I met Peter Ostrum (cast as the lovable Charlie Bucket) on one of the soundstages, and was immediately smitten. In retrospect, I realize that I was anxious about how well the cast would gel, both on- and off-screen. But after meeting Peter, I knew we'd be friends, and this relieved much of my anxiety.

Born in November 1957 in Dallas, Texas, Peter Gardner Ostrum entered the world less than a week later than I. Raised in the small Cleveland, Ohio, suburb of Shaker Heights, a stone's throw from Lake Erie, Peter was a sixth-grader when he was scouted by casting agents during a performance at the Cleveland Play House Children's Theater. The Play House, credited as America's first regional theater, was founded during the vaudevillian era, and its "Curtain Pullers" education program was a magnet for young talent. Paul Newman and Joel Grey (who was also the first actor considered for the role of Willy Wonka) both began their prolific careers at the Play House.

The intensive national casting search for an actor to play Charlie Bucket was led by Marion Dougherty, a prominent Hollywood casting agent, who scoured children's theaters across the nation. Casting agents watched

Peter Ostrum as the lovable "Charlie Bucket". Author Roald Dahl described the Charlie character as "honest, obedient, loyal, trustworthy, brave, good, kind and starving." Peter's heartwarming performance encompassed all of these characteristics. No easy task for a new actor making his first film debut.

53

hundreds of actors in their search for a young boy whose onscreen personality would embody the traits of Dahl's central character. They found all those ingredients and more in Peter Ostrum. It took only a couple of Polaroid snapshots and a recorded reading from Dahl's book to convince Mel Stuart that he had found his Charlie. After a final audition with Mel in New York, during which Peter was asked to sing "My Country, 'Tis of Thee," Peter was offered the role ten days before production began in Germany.

My first meeting with Gene Wilder in the wardrobe department was also memorable. His quiet elegance as well as his gentle and kind nature made him the perfect Willy Wonka. Gene made his film debut in the 1967 Oscar-winning *Bonnie & Clyde*, and his first major role was as Leo Bloom in the 1968 film, *The Producers*, where he quickly established his on-screen versatility. Ultimately, Gene would be best known for his collaborations with writer/director Mel Brooks in a series of hit films that followed *Willy Wonka*. The best description of Gene's portrayal of Willy Wonka was given by David Wolper himself, who later wrote, "Gene Wilder fit the role of Willy Wonka tighter than Jacques Cousteau's wetsuit." That couldn't have been more accurate. It is interesting to note that Paramount Pictures' official *Willie Wonka* press kit mentioned that Gene's father was an importer of Holland chocolates.

Gene was such an amazing person. He had a very gentle and charismatic presence both on-and off screen and all of us kids were constantly vying for his attention. Gene's first film role was in the 1967 classic motion picture *Bonnie and Clyde* where he was cast as Eugene Grizzard, a small but prominent role with Warren Beatty and Faye Dunaway. His first headlining role came only a year later in *The Producers*, a comedy film written and directed by his longtime friend Mel Brooks. His performance was nominated for Best Actor in a Supporting Role by the Academy of Motion Picture Arts and Sciences.

Munich

Just before returning to London having recorded my song, I was invited to another dinner, this time to meet the story's author, Roald Dahl. Even after all these years, I recall being a bit scared of him. He was tall—really, really tall from my vantage point—intimidating, and somewhat forbidding. While he was gracious, he didn't smile much or seem to make any effort to help me feel at ease. It felt more like an interview than a friendly conversation. He was, however, interested in my thoughts and ideas about Veruca, and our discussion concentrated on the character's origins and complexities. I asked him where the name Veruca came from. He said that warts are horrible things, Veruca was a "wart of a girl," and the nastiest place to get warts was on your foot; hence "Veruca." (A plantar wart's scientific name is *Verruca plantaris*.) By the end of dinner, Dahl seemed to warm up a bit, and I listened carefully to his descriptions of the various characters. This proved useful in helping me determine how I would approach Veruca's relationships with the other players. After that evening, my interaction with Dahl was limited to an occasional on-set encounter; we spoke very little from then on.

Mel Stuart tried to shoot the movie as chronologically as possible. During the early production stages, this worked in my favor, as I was allowed to return home for three weeks. I spent this time studying every detail of Veruca. I remember treating my script like a school exercise book, covering it in plastic to protect it. I even made an index and contents page to locate scenes quickly. I rehearsed in my bedroom until I was word perfect.

I also cherished this precious time with my mother and sister, for very soon, I would be returning to Munich where I would be isolated from them for an unimaginable ten weeks—an eternity for a young girl of twelve.

My original handwritten table of contents page which I created for my script. It seems even at this tender age my approach to filming was professional and methodical!

Roy, seen here as "Clapper" in Richard Lester's *How I Won the War* with John Lennon (1967), was a funny, versatile and prolific actor who over the course of his career appeared in over two hundred film, television and stage productions.

The Magic Begins

AFTER JUST THREE WEEKS at home in Guildford, studying every detail of the script and my musical number, I was on my way to rejoin my fellow cast members in bringing Dahl's masterpiece to life onscreen. When Sue and I boarded the plane to return to Munich on September 20, 1970, the day was overcast and gloomy, but it opened one of the sunniest chapters of my life.

It was a heart-wrenching goodbye. I was excited, but so wished that my mother and sister were going with me. The idea of living in a foreign country for such a long time without my family was overwhelming. Though I wanted them to share my experiences in person, they would only hear my stories through letters and an occasional telephone call.

We arrived in Munich, and while waiting to retrieve our luggage, Sue and I recognized Roy Kinnear—cast as my character's adoring father, Henry Salt—and introduced ourselves. Roy, also from England, was already a distinguished actor, and over the duration of our shooting schedule, I came to admire him immensely. He assumed the role of my father not only on-screen, but also during the countless hours between takes. In many ways, his nature off-screen was parallel to his on-screen character. He tried hard to make me laugh and also served as a mentor, giving advice and letting me in on some of his personal acting secrets. Although it sounds clichéd, he truly was like the father I never had.

By the time we met, Roy had already spent what seemed to be a life-time in the arts. As a young man, he had attended the Royal Academy of Dramatic Art in Britain. In 1959, following a variety of stage, radio and minor onscreen roles, he joined Joan Littlewood's Theatre Workshop at the Theatre Royal Stratford East. Coincidently, as a teenager, my grandmother's parents ran the local public house "the Railway Tavern." It was here that my grandmother used to climb down the drain pipe, hitching her skirt up with a piece of string, and sneaked out between the dray horses to the see the variety bill at the Theatre Royal Stratford East and thus began her love affair with band music. Some years later when I was to perform at the same venue, I was told how Roy and his fellow actors who were all somewhat strapped for cash, would sleep at the theatre on the floor of the box suites. Roy performed in the theater and film productions of *Sparrows Can't Sing*, both directed by Littlewood, and soon thereafter, became a household name. His impressive series of roles in both television and film ranged from pro-ductions of *Hamlet* to *Batman* and from wholesome "Walt Disney Presents" to the darker themes of *Count Dracula*. But it was his association with film director and close friend Richard Lester for which he became best known. Their first project together was the 1965 Beatles film, *Help!*; a year later, he starred as a gladiator instructor in Lester's *A Funny Thing Happened on the Way to the Forum*. This was followed with another classic Lester production, *How I Won the War*, in which he co-starred with John Lennon.

Back in Munich, Sue, myself and Roy shared a car back to the Palace Hotel. Upon arrival, I was handed a large envelope containing script chang-es and a set of call sheets outlining our shooting schedule. My first evening back in Munich was uneventful. We had dinner and met for the first time

Opposite: When I first arrived on the set of *Willy Wonka*, I watched in awe as Jack and Peter performed their song and dance number of "I've Got a Golden Ticket." It was the first time I had been able to closely observe the inner-workings of a busy film set. The façade cottage interior along with the two actors, skipping and waltzing around the set, take-after-take, quickly became sobering when I realized that this was going to be a grueling process. But the performance captured on film was every bit as delightful as seeing it in person. They were brilliant in their performance and it was here that I realized I was to be part of a very special movie.

Nora "Dodo" Denney, who was cast as Mrs. Teevee. My first impression of Dodo was positive—she was very sweet and seemed to fit the character perfectly. Dodo's background was diverse; she was not only an actor but also an accomplished artist. She began her career in television with her own show, *Marilynn the Witch*, for KCMO-TV, in Kansas City, Missouri, in the late 1950s. When not hosting her Saturday evening program, she could be seen giving advice on topics ranging from gardening to cooking. Her zany comedic characters were to become popular fixtures in television series ranging from *Bewitched* to *My Favorite Martian*.

The following morning, I was driven to the studio, where I was taken to wardrobe for my final costume fittings. Mel Stuart appeared, and—after advising that my sleeves were too tight and my coat would also need to be taken up a bit—gave approval. I was then invited to the soundstage where they were filming Peter Ostrum and Jack Albertson's classic song-and-dance scene, "I've Got a Golden Ticket."

I had never been on a working film set during a production, and it was quite a revelation to see what a busy operation it was. I entered the interior sets of the Bucket cottage, where crewman were pulling long cables, massive lighting arrays were being set into position, the cinematographer was

carefully measuring emulsion exposures, and the actors were in position awaiting the director's call for action. I was caught completely off guard by how real the cottage appeared. In my innocence, I expected the cottage to have four walls and was amazed to see that it had only three in order to accommodate the camera.

At Mel's cue, the exuberant musical track to "I've Got a Golden Ticket" blared through large speakers fed from a reel-to-reel tape recorder. The cheerful music permeated every space of the soundstage. I was dazzled as Peter and Jack danced and crisscrossed the set with what looked like unrestrained glee. But the realities of filmmaking became apparent as Mel, seeking absolute perfection, demanded take after take, again and again and then once more, until every choreographed movement was precise to script.

This was also my first meeting with the wonderful and talented Jack Albertson. Jack, a seasoned song-and-dance and comedic skit veteran of the vaudeville stage, was already an icon in American film by this time. He had worked with all the greats, including Jimmy Durante, Jack Benny, Milton Berle, and Red Skelton, and won an Academy Award in 1968 for Best Supporting Actor in the motion picture,

Jack Albertson (Grandpa Joe) had transcended the entire spectrum of entertainment by the time he arrived on the set of *Willy Wonka*. The year prior he won an Academy Award for his work in the motion picture *The Subject was Roses*, and all of us were immediately drawn to him. He became a close friend and mentor to all of us during the production. His work as an entertainer dates back to vaudevillian roots in the 1930s. Jack was an incredibly versatile comedian, dancer, singer, and musician in television, film, stage and radio. His work was far reaching and it included everything from comedy varieties to intense political dramas and blazing westerns. He covered the entire realm of entertainment. For Jack's work in television, he was honored with a star on the Hollywood Walk of Fame. He was a very special personality and much of the heart of the film is owed to Jack.

Jack as "Grandpa Joe" on the cottage set with Peter Ostrum as "Charlie Bucket."

Denise Nickerson (seen here as Amy Jennings in the 1960s daytime series *Dark Shadows*) was cast as the gum-chewing Violet Beauregarde and was already considered a seasoned actress when she landed her role in *Willy Wonka*. Denise was the oldest of the child actors and had appeared in a variety of popular television programs including *Flipper* and *The Jackie Gleason Show*. Denise later went on to appear in numerous television series including episodes of *Walt Disney Presents* and *The Brady Bunch*.

I Want it Now!

The Subject Was Roses. Nonetheless, he was always charming, modest and unassuming, and he made the experience so enjoyable.

I still remember him leaning in to introduce himself with his charming soft drawl: "Hello...How are ya, kid?" I have only the fondest memories of this wonderful man, who was sweet to everyone and had a lot of patience working with us youngsters. As production went on, he kept us amused with his repertoire of old vaudevillian routines, twirling his hat and cane and doing other bits of visual comedy. Working with him was a real gift.

It was also during this visit that I met some of the other actors, including Denise Nickerson, who was cast as Violet Beauregarde, and Paris Themmen, cast as Mike Teevee. Denise and I were the same age and became very close— almost like sisters—during the production. Even today, we still call each other "sis." As time went on, we spent a lot of our free time together in our hotel rooms chewing gum, listening to music, reading books, and talking about almost everything. I was slightly in awe of her, although the same age as me, she seemed very sophisticated and was already a seasoned actor. Cast as Amy Collins in a very popular American television series, *Dark Shadows*, she seemed completely comfortable with the environment of the busy film set.

Paris, though a talented actor, was a completely different story. He attended a professional performing school in New York and had appeared on Broadway in the stage productions of *Mame* and *Iphigenia in Aulis*. He still holds a special place in my heart, bless him, but he was only eleven, which at our young age was a huge difference. To put it bluntly, he was annoying, loud, and obnoxious (sorry, Paris, but you were). Many years later, he admitted that he was a bit of a troublemaker during the production. Gene Wilder, in a television interview that took place during filming, offered a humorous but revealing perspective:

Interviewer: How do you like working with the younger generation?

Wilder: Who do you mean by younger generation? You mean the kids?

Interviewer: The little tiny ones, yes…

Wilder: Ah, four of them are fantastic, and one of them I'm going to shoot in the head tomorrow.

Despite his antics, I still enjoyed working with Paris, and he was and still is a dear friend. Interacting with Michael Böllner, cast as the unforgettable Augustus Gloop, was a bit more difficult. Though all of us liked Michael, he spoke only German, and this isolated him during the long filming periods. (Today, Michael speaks excellent English and we all have a wonderful relationship with him.)

After watching the various takes and retakes of the "I've Got a Golden Ticket" scene, our driver, Max, offered to take me to see the Schloss Hotel, to which Peter, Denise and I would be relocated. When I returned to the Palace Hotel, I sat on my bed and wrote to my mother and sister, describing the events of the day and the Schloss Hotel.

The hotel is gorgeous. There is an old castle right next to it, and the outside cafe overlooks a gorgeous valley with a river and trees. It's lovely, so we're moving in there on October the 8th.

Paris Themmen as television's greatest fan, Mike TeeVee.

Welcoming Wonka

REHEARSALS for the exterior factory scenes began on September 22; this was one of the film's pivotal scenes, as the audience's introduction to *Willy Wonka* would define the flow and mystery of each scene thereafter. Set in front of the factory gates, various façades were added to transform the exterior of the Munich Gas Works into Willy Wonka's incredible Chocolate Factory.

The filming of the factory exteriors began on September 23, 1970, the production's eighteenth day of shooting. In this scene, the five Golden Ticket winners arrive to meet Willy Wonka and then make their grand entrance into the factory. There were nearly three hundred supporting artists cast as onlookers, television reporters, city officials, police, photographers, and even a brass band—all to witness the spectacular entrance into Wonka's magnificent Chocolate Factory. I was picked up from my hotel at 6:50 a.m. and had a set call at 7:50 a.m. for makeup. This was my very first day's filming, and the excitement was palpable. For most of us, it was also the first scene filmed with our "parents"; Peter and Jack, however, had already been working together in production. It was a special bonding time as well, as each film parent ostentatiously took on their respective roles, even between takes.

I Want it Now!

This was new territory for many of us, since even during rehearsals, we hadn't seen Gene's entrance as Willy Wonka, and it also marked the first time we'd seen each other in full costume. I felt sorry for Peter—he'd have to wear that dreary costume for the next three months, as would Denise her red hat; for that matter, I wasn't particularly fond of my own hat. On the other hand, my costume included a custom-tailored mink coat, which at the time was considered to be very extravagant and reserved for members of high society.

On our first day of shooting, we had many hours of down time. Roy kept me amused between takes; we talked about our lives and families, and he shared some of his fantastic acting stories. He was a wonderful mentor, and gave me tips to hone my craft. Each phase of this scene was complicated since, no matter what graphical element was being filmed, we had to continue acting as we could be seen in the background of both the close- and wide-angle shots.

Roy taught me my first little acting trick. Though it was cold, the sun was extremely bright, and when the lights were directed at me for my close-ups,

The five lucky ticket winners being escorted by Willy Wonka into the Chocolate Factory.

(Above) While on-location in Germany, I purchased an instamatic camera to take snapshots and share with my mother and sister all of the wondrous experiences of filming a major motion picture. These personal photos were taken during the first days of filming at the Munich Gas Works; the imaginary setting for Willy Wonka's fantastical Chocolate Factory.

(Below, left) With Peter and Denise outside the façade entrance to Wonka's factory. Next to me is my movie script which I carried with me everywhere during production. This was a very exciting period for all of us, and it was here that we all spent time getting to know one another.

(Below right) Family members of the cast, including Peter's mother Sari (seated on the bench - left) and Leonard Stone's wife Carol (seated in Peter's chair), relaxing while filming the exterior shots of Wonka's factory.

A personal snapshot of me in my full Veruca Salt wardrobe at the factory entrance. Note that I am also holding my Golden Ticket.

I couldn't help but squint my eyes. Roy taught me that by closing them and pointing my face towards the light, I would be able to open my eyes for a few vital seconds without blinking on the call of ACTION. He also had this funny little technique that he called his "Left Hand Loomer." As though he was letting me in on the secret of the century, he told me, "When you're standing next to somebody and it's their close-up, you just lean your weight to the left or to the right, just to make sure your shoulder is in their shot. It means that you get in the shot longer, you get more close-ups, you get more cutaways, and you might even get some overtime!" If you watch the film closely, especially during scenes with Gene Wilder, you'll probably see Roy's shoulder always on the edge of frame. I loved learning those bits from him.

One of my special memories of Roy involves a poem that he used to say for me in his best Scottish accent as though it were a song. I begged him over and over and over again to recite it during the hours of tedium and he never refused:

Now you've heard of Hiawatha?
If ye have nae, do nae bother,
You can read it in the 'Wizard' for yourself,
And his wee wife Mini Ha Ha, ha ha ha ha. . . .

The idea for Willy Wonka's entrance originated with Gene Wilder. In the original script versions, when Wonka was first introduced to the audience, he was to perform a "funny little skipping dance" quickly across the courtyard and then, arriving at the gate, simply tip his top-hat and bow. But this

My mother and sister were unable to chaperon me during the production, and I would write to them often with all of the latest news. Long distance telephone calls from Germany to England were extremely expensive during that era and daily phone calls were not possible based on my family's low income and my meager salary. My primary means for communication were letters and postcards and I so enjoyed receiving these packages from my mother which often contained comic books and bubble gum. These letters and postcards were my only connection to home.

didn't work for Gene. During his early discussions with Mel Stuart, he made it a condition of his taking the part that when making his first appearance, he would emerge from the factory with a cane and walk with a slow limp towards a puzzled and silent crowd. Then, just before reaching the gate, he would pretend to stumble but finish this with a spectacular and surprising somersault. Gene's theory was that this would make it hard for the audience to know if he was lying or telling the truth. Willy Wonka needed to be enigmatic, and with this bit of trickery, he succeeded.

My scene entering the gate and my line when meeting Willy Wonka for the first time—"I'm Veruca Salt!"—was captured in just a few takes. The building entrance to the Chocolate Factory was a façade structure; walking through the entry and past the magically opening door (the "magic" courtesy of a kneeling stagehand) simply led to another opening that, if you weren't careful, would bring you back into the shot. On one of the initial takes, I didn't realize this and walked back right into view. But that wasn't my most memorable mistake of the day. During our catered lunch in the Munich Gas Works cafeteria, I hung my precious mink coat on the back of my chair, and then managed to forget it. When we returned to the film set, one of the crew members asked me why I didn't have my coat? Panic struck as I had realized what I had done. Lucky for me, it was exactly where I had left it, and we were able to resume filming without any delay.

Now, nearly four decades later, I still remember that day. I treasure the memory of Roy whispering that special poem to me, and the magic of seeing Gene Wilder emerge as Willy Wonka for the first time. It was also here that I remember signing my very first autograph for a supporting cast member. My life was forever changed after passing through those gates.

When it was time to begin filming the interior scenes, we returned to the soundstages on the lot of the Bavarian Film Studios. Though whenever possible, or at least whenever practical, the film was shot in chronological sequence, some of the initial scenes were not filmed until much later in the production. The scene in which I find my Golden Ticket in the Peanut Factory was actually filmed towards the end of my shooting schedule.

Our next scenes took place in what were known in the script as Room #1, the room with the human-hand coat hangers and the revealing of the contract before entering the factory, and Room #3 (on script, Room #2 was eliminated). Room #3 was a small façade room with wooden walls painted to resemble the convoluted patterns of M. C. Escher. This was the first scene filmed and it proved to be a challenge—it was very uncomfortable for all us. Just as it appears on film, the spaced was terribly cramped. I remember the painful moment, when, my ear smashed against the wall, and I forgot my line, "Let me out or I'll scream." Mel began to shout, "Cut! Cut! Cut! Who should have been speaking?" It was me. Leonard Stone, cast as Sam Beauregarde, quickly came to my defense when I started to cry, but Mel was not moved, and made it clear that this was completely unacceptable. (During the taping of our commentary in a New York studio for the thirtieth anniversary DVD release, even Peter Ostrum remembered my forgotten-line experience.)

Our scene in Room #3, the dead-end-hallway, cramped and terribly uncomfortable to film which was intended to be reminiscent of a carnival funhouse.

Mel Stuart ran the set with formality and expected the actors to be prepared. He had little tolerance for mediocrity, and there were many hurt feelings when a performance wasn't up to the caliber he desired. This is not to say that he wasn't kind, and I certainly hold a special place in my heart for Mel, but his exacting expectations were not always sensitive to the emotions of young actors. I had been brought up in a proper English household and found Mel frightening and intimidating. In his presence, the entire crew walked on eggshells as he paced, his trademark lens dangling from a cord around his neck. He was fast-talking and sharp-tongued when people crossed him or didn't follow his direction. I have vivid memories of hearing him screaming "God damn it!" clear across the set. However, I didn't miss my cues during any of the subsequent takes that day (or any other!).

In Room #1, they had kept the human hands as hangers a secret to capture our spontaneous reactions. While we all had an idea of what was to come, it was still fun to have some element of mystery. I don't recall ever seeing any of the support crew on the other side of the wall, and their identities remain secret. I was more interested in finally getting rid of my detested hat. In this particular scene my line to Roy of "You're always making things difficult!" has long remained one of my favorites. On the wall-size contract was shrinking calligraphy, which I later learned was the product of Hank Wynands' wife, Nancy. Hank was one of the creative geniuses in charge of set construction. The signature sections of the contract were patched with Velcro and replaced with a blank for each new take. I recall being quite impressed by the forethought and crafty ingenuity of this prop design. The largest soundstage holding the Chocolate Room was now nearing completion, and what we were about to see was beyond our wildest dreams.

INT. THE CHOCOLATE ROOM—FULL SHOT

A VAST COUNTRY LANDSCAPE. The MEADOW in which they stand slopes gently downward toward a great river. The meadow-grass is GREEN and dotted with small wild flowers of EVERY COLOR. There are tall TREES of weird fantastic shapes, shrubs, flowers, little paths. Everything in brilliant curious colors. The great RIVER below in the cleft of the valley (too far off to occupy the children's immediate attention) is BROWN, and at the head of the river is a high WATERFALL down which the brown 'water' crashes and tumbles into a boiling whirlpool. Below the river, are ENORMOUS GLASS PIPES. Each roughly three feet in diameter. These pipes appear BROWN because they are filled with the brown 'water' from the river. In the distance, the river disappears into a MIST. Along the banks of the river there are weeping willows and alders, brilliant flowers. Into this incredible room dances Mr. WONKA followed by FULL GROUP and we immediately go into the PRODUCTION NUMBER—THE MAGIC SONG.

I Want it Now!

Deep beyond the entrance gate to Willy Wonka's factory, shrouded in secrecy, was the most important room of all; the Chocolate Room. A mysterious and marvelous confectionary utopia, a colorful interior world filled with wonder and sweet marvel. Most of the actors hadn't seen the Chocolate Room prior to filming, and even my brief peek didn't prepare me for the sheer magnitude of this set. The Chocolate Room soundstage was situated inside a massive stadium like structure. Our dressing rooms were located upstairs, and on the first day of filming the Chocolate Room scene, the corridors were overflowing with excitement.

This was an era before computer-generated animation, and the Chocolate Room was a world seen in only places like Disneyland. As crews readied the set, we waited behind the giant door, trying to contain our excitement.

Ladies and Gentlemen...Boys and Girls...The Chocolate Room...

Opposite: A candid photo of Gene during the filming of his Pu
Imagination musical number. The arm of a stage hand can be se
holding the tree that Gene is leaning again

Pure Imagination

Then finally, with cameras rolling and on the director's cue, the large door opened to reveal the most magical place I'd ever seen. As I entered, the cascading sound of the chocolate waterfall could be heard, and the vibrant candy-colored scenery was dazzling. Even decades later, the bright colors are vivid in my memory, and I recall scanning the room from corner to corner in pure wonderment. We performed only a couple of takes to capture our entrance, and I am certain that the one used in the film was the first.

The Chocolate Room scene took several days to film. I loved watching Gene perform his memorable "Pure Imagination" song and dance number. Gene and Howard Jeffrey had choreographed the way in which Willy Wonka would lead us down the steps and into the factory. We had never rehearsed this scene, and the only direction that Mel offered was that we were never to walk ahead of Gene. Denise and I pushed and shoved each other as we progressed down each step, ad-libbing each take. I recall getting struck at least a couple of times by Gene's cane, and can still hear his soft voice singing "Pure Imagination" under the amplified master track as he lip-synched to his own recording. It was during this number that we really became in awe of the man cast in the role of Willy Wonka.

To a greater degree than most, Gene had isolated himself from us prior to filming the Chocolate Room scenes, but from this point forward, we all began to spend more time together and I adored being around him. He was a brilliant and animated storyteller with a wonderful sense of humor. There were a variety of technical complexities within the Chocolate Room set that sometimes translated into long periods of down time while things like the waterfall and lighting were adjusted. Gene kept us enthralled, and

it was not uncommon to find one of us kids sitting on his lap and begging him to tell another joke or fanciful tale. The privilege to be the chosen one to sit on his lap became quite a competition.

During the "Pure Imagination" segment, we were given Wonka's consent to venture out and sample the sweet candy terrain. But despite my character's quest for a lifetime supply of chocolate, in reality, I hated it. In one shot, Veruca was required to smash a polystyrene watermelon against a rock and then scoop the gooey chocolate by hand to devour its contents greedily. The taste of this runny-textured chocolate gloop was so disgusting that I could barely force myself to eat it, much less pretend that I was enjoying it. Mel was screaming through his bullhorn: "Come on, Julie, act like you're enjoying it!" and I would snap back: "But I'm NOT enjoying it!" By the time this scene was completed, I felt ill from ingesting this chocolate-flavored nastiness.

Though chocolate wasn't my favorite candy fare, I still enjoyed our daily spoils. There were times when we exchanged candy as if we had just returned from a Halloween event. I remember Paris, his pockets bursting at the seams with gumballs, and the fun we had while sitting in our dressing rooms trading and eating our sugary treats. We sometimes were able to leverage our relationship with the prop men, who allowed us to sample their edible creations or passed along some of our favorite treats before placing them as stage props.

One of my very special memories is of a small "inventing room" just off the main set. I thoroughly enjoyed peeking into it and catching glimpses of the props mens' masterful creations. Everything we ate was designed here, and we were keen to volunteer as tasters. I recall them snipping off the ears of a teddy bear and replacing them with a sweetened gel candy that Denise would savor onscreen. I also remember watching them pour wax into molds to create the buttercups, the only "eatable" item that was inedible. At the finale of "Pure Imagination," Gene holds one of these buttercups and bites off a piece, chewing it in delight. But when the camera stopped rolling and "Cut" was broadcast, Gene spat it out. The prop men replaced it with a new one for the next take.

Filming the various scenes inside the Chocolate Room was accomplished over the course of several weeks, and it was here that we really started to bond with one another, both on and off the set, often enjoying meals and weekends together. It was also becoming apparent that I was developing a crush on Peter, but so was Denise. While Denise and I were extremely close, a rivalry developed as we both vied for Peter's attention. I wrote to my family describing one of our first outings together in late September. My interest in Peter even at this early stage was clearly evident:

Dear Mummy, Lynn, Nana & Carol,

Well I've been here a week now and I'm longing to come home. Thank you for my card, gum, sweets, book, comics, letters (Gosh there's so much to thank you for!) Where shall I begin . . . Ummm. The October Fest was lovely. Denise (Violet), Peter (Charlie), Bob Roe (the Assistant Director's son & Peter's stand-in) and I met and went together. Peter's Mum, Sue and Pattie (who is Denise's sister and chaperone), came with us and let us go round the fair on our own. For the first time that I can remember anyway, I went on a Roller Coaster. I enjoyed it so much, I went on it at least 20 times. One roller coaster went down at a 75 degree angle. That reminds me, I must go back to fetch my stomach, I left it behind (boom, boom). The Ferris Wheel nearly made me ill because we stopped at the top. Ouch! We all had reserved seats in a beer hall there because the company had invited everyone. It was great! Hic! Hic! Now what makes you think I drank beer? Yeah and guess who was in the queue for the loo afterwards?

Peter asked me to go on a ride with him. Peter is the only nice one. We went for walk down by the river the other day and it was lovely. I have got to record my song again for the musical arranger. Apparently this is always done for musicals. I'm doing it on Friday evening. Next time you write, (if you can bear to) I think it might be best to write to the Schloss. The price ranges from 35 marks to 68 per night. Ours is 45 with a bath & loo. I've been rehearsing my song today, the new version, and also filming the "Pure Imagination" one in the Chocolate Room today. Carol (who is Leonard's wife who is Sam Beauregarde) thinks this might be another Wizard of Oz, but anyway we'll have to see. Roy's wife has the code number for Germany so if I gave it to you it would be cheaper than me ringing you if I sent you the money. Oh yes, I have not got the receipts done yet, but I've saved 8 pounds this week so I will try to send it to you. Must go now, the match sticks for my eyes have now snapped. No, I'm not tired really (yawn, yawn).

All my (yawn) love,
Julie

Although I had a sneaky peek at the Oompa Loompas costumes and wigs in the wardrobe department, this was the first time any of us had seen them for real. Our reactions on-film are wholly authentic. We were all caught off guard by how amazing they looked in character. But these cast members, had the toughest acting jobs of all of us. They were first to arrive in the early morning hours of the production and the last to leave. They endured long hours in the makeup suites that resulted in layered makeup that was touched-up constantly throughout their shooting schedule. Much of the time they sat idle with white bibs around their necks to prevent the makeup from getting on their clothing. I truly felt sorry for them, despite their reputations of being a hard partying bunch that often closed down the pubs in Munich each night (or at least it was rumored).

Gene Wilder with the Oompa Loompa cast. British actor Rusty Goff (L), the youngest of the Oompa Loompa players, was designated as the lead actor and has had a very prolific acting career in mega hit films that range from *Star Wars* to the *Harry Potter* series.

Back on the set and finishing up the "Pure Imagination" musical scenes, we saw for the first time all of the Oompa Loompas at work on the other side of the river. While I had seen one of them in full costume, as well as several of their green wigs lined up in the makeup suite, nothing had prepared me for the sight of all of them in character, adding ingredients to the chocolate river.

Reminiscent of the Munchkin and Lollipop Guild members in the *Wizard of Oz*, the Oompa Loompa actors were among the toughest cast members to recruit. Rusty Goffe, who, though the youngest, became the lead actor of this group, later commented that they had a very difficult time locating actors with the physical characteristics needed for these roles. Mel Stuart later said that several of the actors had been circus performers, recruited from London, Munich, Turkey, and even Malta. The actors playing the Oompa Loompas endured long hours in the makeup chair, heavy green wigs that were hot and uncomfortable under the bright studio lamps, and continual touch-ups of what became caked-on makeup; by the end of the day, the powder could almost be peeled off in layers.

I am told that some of the Oompa Loompas had rather scandalous reputations, and had been known to party rather hard. But my own memories were mostly sympathetic, knowing how difficult their days must have been in those costumes and makeup. Called first and released last, they spent long hours on the set, usually beginning with dawn call times for makeup and costume fitting. In between takes, the makeup crew converged upon the Oompa Loompas, fitting them with bib-style collar napkins to keep the makeup from spotting their white pants and suspenders. Since they came from a variety of European countries, not all of them spoke English or even had a common language, and they were mostly directed by hand gestures. Today, watching their scenes, little evidence of any difficulty can be seen. Even their lip-synching to the Oompa Loompa music while performing dance numbers was such high-caliber work that one would never know the challenges they faced during production.

I enjoyed their performances, and during filming breaks, would sit on the river edge, close to the waterfall, and enjoy my lunch while they played the prerecorded tracks of "Pure Imagination" and "Oompa Loompa" over the loud speakers, rehearsing and establishing camera angles as technicians scurried about, tinkering and making adjustments to mechanical gear. It was like visiting an enchanted forest.

Michael Böllner's scene as the unforgettable Augustus Gloop was the next one we tackled in the Chocolate Room. The language barrier limited our interactions to simple hellos, smiles, and nods, but little beyond that. Michael had no prior acting experience; his mother had responded to a local newspaper advertisement seeking a young actor who could fit the bill as the stout and greedy Augustus Gloop. Michael lived about thirty minutes from the film studio and more than thirty years later, I learned that he was the only one of us without a dressing room. In between takes, he usually kept to himself or ventured around the set on his own.

Michael's character was the first lucky ticket holder to meet his demise in Wonka's factory. In Michael's scene, his character Augustus quietly sneaks down to the edge of the chocolate river and samples what is described in Dahl's book as "hot melted chocolate" by scooping it into his mouth as fast as he could. As Wonka feebly pleads with Augustus to stop because he is contaminating the entire chocolate supply, the oblivious boy leans even farther over the edge, then falls into the river and cannot be saved.

With the help of our dialogue coach, Frawley Becker, and assistant director, Wolfgang Glattes, who was fluent in German, Michael was directed to fall into the river over a series of nearly forty takes or so he claims! He only had one set of costumes and had to remain in his cold, wet lederhosen for the entire day.

Pure Imagination

The river was only about a foot deep, with a small square section that was about four to five feet deep. This was where Michael had to aim his fall for safety. The special effects team used chemical dyes along with a milk powder to create the chocolate appearance and textures seen on film. Crewmen worked feverously to maintain its consistency, and on at least one occasion, the water had to be drained when the color shifted to a reddish hue and gave off a foul musty smell that permeated the entire soundstage.

These were our last interactions with Michael. Because we were not required to be on-set during his cutaway scenes, I missed seeing the filming of these segments. The scene in which Augustus was blasted through the glass tube was accomplished with a lifelike mannequin crafted from Michael's measurements. The mannequin looked almost real even from our standpoint. Our group of five was now down to four. Michael's character, along with Mrs. Gloop (played by German actress Ursula Reit), wrapped filming after completion of these scenes, and we parted with only a simple goodbye. Michael never returned to the set, and his quick, low-key departure resonated amongst the rest of us, reminding us that this fantastical journey wasn't going to last forever, and that each of our numbers would be coming up soon enough.

Michael didn't see any of the remaining scenes until the official release the following year. Along with the rest of the movie-going public, he attended a local premiere and had his first glimpse of his own scenes in their final edited form. It would be nearly thirty years before we would connect with Michael again.

Our cast watching the demise of Golden Ticket number one winner Augustus Gloop. In truth, it was heartrending for us when Michael's character met his gluttonous fate by falling into the chocolate river. It symbolized that each one of our characters were soon to meet our end, and then it would be back to normality.

Standing with Roy and his wife Carmel in front of the Schloss Hotel.

Home Away from Home

ASMALL HOTEL with storybook charm nestled in the southern countryside of Grünwald, with picturesque views of the Bavarian Alps, became a home away from home for Peter and his mother, Denise and her sister Pattie, our dialogue coach Frawley Becker (who traveled with his "movie cat" Calvados), and me and my chaperone Sue Breen for the rest of the filming. Set within a multicultural quarter of fine dining and bistros, the Schloss hotel was a nine-bedroom lodge reminiscent of an intimate bed and breakfast. It was here that we spent our evenings and weekends when not filming, and it continues to be a place full of special memories for me even decades later. The interior was traditional Bavarian style, with antique furnishings and uneven wooden floors that spoke of its long and well-used past. It was the only place we were allowed to run free and spend unsupervised time together. The ground-level terrace overlooked the Isar River, and this was one of the few places we were unguarded and able to be kids.

The Isar, which drains the Bavarian Alps and eventually makes its way to the Black Sea, was a majestic sight. Even at my young age, I sensed the deeply rooted history of the region. Munich, in southeastern Germany near

Snapshot photos of Denise and me taken during one of our weekend breaks along the Isar River. Peter, Denise and I spent countless hours on the weekends exploring the river bank outside our hotel. It was a very special place for us as it was the only time that we were able to relax and behave like normal kids.

the Bavarian Alps, was founded in 1158 and had long been the center of Bavaria. Adolf Hitler organized the German Workers' Party (later to become the National Socialist German Workers' Party, or Nazi for short) here after World War I, and it was also here that the Munich Agreement was signed in 1938, annexing Czechoslovakia and making it part of Germany. Following heavy Allied bombardment during World War II, the city was largely rebuilt.

Peter's room was on the top floor and had a panoramic view of the Alps; my room also had a spectacular view of the mountains and river. We had no televisions, and nearly all of the printed matter available was in German, which meant that we were dependent on things sent from home. I savored the magazines and comics my mother mailed to me, as these were my only connection to England. Roy and myself were in the minority as we were the only two Brits in this American – German collaboration. Even though we were only a two-hour flight from London, it felt like we were worlds away.

We "Wonka kids" usually ate together in the downstairs restaurant, where we discovered the hotel's wonderful sugary desserts. Our favorite was the

Bavarian Surprise, which we practically lived on. It was a kind of version of a baked Alaska, a huge concoction of meringue, fruit and ice cream that was then baked in the oven. We also challenged one another's' tolerance for the more unpleasant-sounding fare, such as garlic snails (escargot) and frogs' legs. Each time, we set the ante a bit higher than the last. My favorite dish, which I ordered practically every night, was baked chicken in a flavorful mushroom crème sauce; I was also partial to the fresh trout that was fished from the river below and was the hotel specialty.

My interest in Peter continued to blossom, and I cherished spending quiet time with him along the river. On weekends, we took long walks together looking for smooth, flat stones to skip on the water's surface. Peter was intent on showing me how to select and then throw the stones just right and make them bounce; however, my interest was more in the teacher than in the lesson. (I never did master the art, much to Peter's amusement some thirty years later when we revisited Munich.) We also explored the surroundings. These exciting and sometimes adventurous expeditions were a great escape from the intense atmosphere of the set. During one of these

Denise and I practicing "skipping stones" on the Isar. Despite Peter's best teaching efforts, neither of us ever accomplished this.

Bobby Roe, the son of Assistant Director Jack Roe and stand-in for Peter (although he did have a brief speaking part as Peter Goff in the classroom scenes), was also one of our very close friends during the production. His father was a very kind presence around the set and was another seasoned veteran of Hollywood. He had worked as the assistant director on blockbuster films like *Funny Girl* with Barbara Streisand to a long string of series television ranging from *The Adventures of Ozzie and Harriet* to the grand episodic westerns of *The Big Valley*.

outings, Peter found a World War II- German soldier's helmet (which he still has today) along the riverbed. These finds made our journeys that much more exciting. Peter and I became very close during these walks, and would talk for hours on end about everything. While our relationship was never to become romantic, Peter was my first crush, and I cherished every minute we were together alone. But as it turned out, I wasn't the only one vying for his attention.

All of us were close in age and on the brink of teenage-hood. It soon became apparent that Denise had also set her sights on Peter, and a rivalry emerged that was sometimes acted out even on the set. As Denise later commented, "There was only one of him and two of us; it made it a little difficult." In an unspoken arrangement, we used to take turns sitting next to him. If one was more successful than the other in getting Peter's attention, we would often avoid each other. This rivalry continued throughout the shooting schedule, but most of the time, Denise and I enjoyed one another's company and spent endless hours together in our hotel rooms, talking and listening to music.

Denise and her older sister, Pattie, who doubled as her chaperone, had brought with them a small collection of LPs that included some of the teenage heartthrobs of the era. We delighted in sitting on our beds, chewing gum and singing along to artists like David Cassidy with hits from the *Partridge Family Album*, including "I Think I Love You," "I Really Want to Know You," and "I Can Feel Your Heartbeat"; Simon & Garfunkel's unforgettable "Bridge Over Troubled Water," and Bobby Sherman's 1970 hit, "Julie, Do

Home Away from Home

You Love Me?" among many others. We gossiped about trendy topics during some of our shopping adventures in town. My mother sent me the latest copies of *Bunty* and *Judy*, comic books that often included a surprise pack, usually gum or temporary tattoos. I anxiously awaited her packages, with their news from home and fun-filled reading. Long-distance phone calls, which were terribly expensive, were out of the question. I was only able to call home once a week if I was lucky. International calls had to be booked and on my mother's wages were beyond our budget.

On a few occasions, I was invited to the homes of Mel Stuart and the assistant director, Jack Roe, whose son Bobby served as Peter Ostrum's stand-in and who also had a brief role as Peter Goff (the boy in the classroom scene who professes that he's opened "a hundred and fifty" Wonka bars). Madeline Stuart, the initial influence for *Willy Wonka and the Chocolate Factory* as a motion picture, became a good friend during the production. Both Madeline and her brother, Peter, were given small parts in the film. In the classroom scene, Madeline appears as Madeline Durkin and Peter as Winkelmann; Peter also appears in the early scenes inside the candy shop during the memorable musical number, "The Candy Man," sung by Aubrey Woods (as Bill, the candy store owner). Madeline and I got along well; we explored the English Gardens together and also had fun just playing at the

Madeline the daughter of *Willy Wonka's* Director Mel Stuart, was the true inspiration behind the movie. It was her love for Dahl's classic book that persuaded her father to bring the tale to the silver screen. Madeline and I (seen here at the English Gardens in Munich) remained good friends throughout the production and spent a lot of time together during our shooting breaks. Madeline also enjoyed a small role as Madeline Durkin in the classroom scene along with her brother Peter who played Winklemann.

Stuart's location home. One of our games involved taking cork-style circular coasters and sticking toothpicks into the sides, then tossing them at each other like Frisbees. Mel quickly intervened, but not out of concern for me, I suspect he was calculating the cost of a halt in production if one of these homemade weapons hit its target.

But the weeks away from home grew long for this twelve-year-old, and I missed my mother and sister terribly. The other children had at least one family member to keep them company. Peter was with his mother, Sari; Denise, with her sister Pattie; and Paris was with his mother at a different hotel. To add to the strain, while the other kids had entire weekends off, on Saturdays, I was usually driven back to the studio, where Howard Jeffrey and I rehearsed the choreography of my musical number over and over until we achieved perfection. What looks spontaneous onscreen was in fact planned down to the smallest detail.

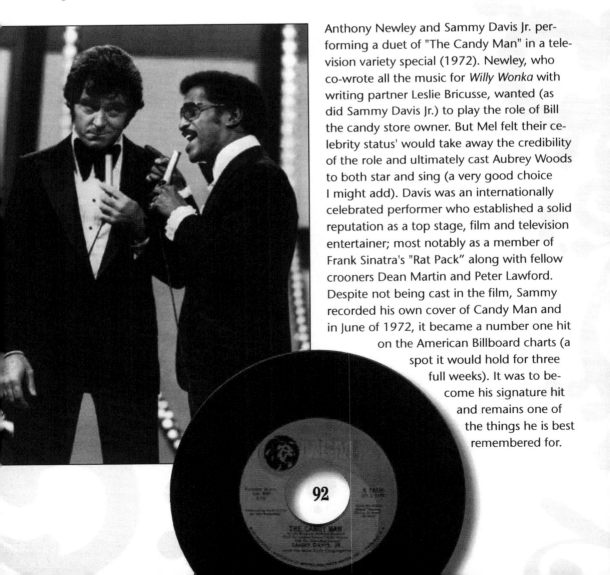

Anthony Newley and Sammy Davis Jr. performing a duet of "The Candy Man" in a television variety special (1972). Newley, who co-wrote all the music for *Willy Wonka* with writing partner Leslie Bricusse, wanted (as did Sammy Davis Jr.) to play the role of Bill the candy store owner. But Mel felt their celebrity status' would take away the credibility of the role and ultimately cast Aubrey Woods to both star and sing (a very good choice I might add). Davis was an internationally celebrated performer who established a solid reputation as a top stage, film and television entertainer; most notably as a member of Frank Sinatra's "Rat Pack" along with fellow crooners Dean Martin and Peter Lawford. Despite not being cast in the film, Sammy recorded his own cover of Candy Man and in June of 1972, it became a number one hit on the American Billboard charts (a spot it would hold for three full weeks). It was to become his signature hit and remains one of the things he is best remembered for.

From Script to Screen

BY THE TIME *Willy Wonka* started production in 1970, Roald Dahl was already a seasoned screenwriter. He had started his writing career with a short story he sold to the *Saturday Evening Post* in 1941. In the story, he recounted the adventure he had during World War II while serving as a fighter pilot in the Royal Air Force. He later said that he found his niche when his stories became "less realistic and more fictional." Even in some of his earliest works of adult literature, Dahl's characters comprised ominous and yet somehow amusing traits that endlessly intrigued his readers.

His most famous and critically analyzed short story, "Lamb to the Slaughter," published in *Collier's Magazine* in 1953, illustrates this perfectly. The central character, Mary Maloney, six months pregnant and content with her ordinary but satisfying life, is shocked when her husband, a police officer, tells her that he intends to end their marriage. Reacting impulsively, Mary bludgeons her husband to death with a frozen leg of lamb, and then devises an elaborate alibi. Upon being questioned by the police, she prepares and serves them the murder weapon. Crafting stories filled with dark characters and charming personalities earned Dahl his reputation as a master of the unexpected. He later expanded into television, writing for a variety of mystery theater programs, including six episodes for *Alfred Hitchcock Presents* that aired between 1958 and 1961. Dahl also had an intuitive insight into the boundless imaginations of children, and a knack for capturing the world as seen through their eyes. The characters he created were so timeless that today, children still flock to his gravesite to leave gifts of chocolate and celebrate his work.

In 1960, with his writing career thriving, Dahl purchased a new home and moved his family to the south of England, to the Buckinghamshire village of Great Missenden. For his writing quarters, Dahl preferred the isolation of a small shed at the bottom of his garden, and it was here that he crafted *Charlie and the Chocolate Factory*. Dahl had a gift for bringing not only the human characters to life, but also giving personalities to the gadgetry featured in his stories. In 1967, Dahl was hired to adapt Ian Fleming's charming children's novel, *Chitty Chitty Bang Bang*, for the screen. *Chitty Chitty Bang Bang*'s characters have many parallels in Dahl's own work, and its magical gadgetry, sweet confections and imaginary worlds were well-known territory to him as well. This experience served to further develop the characters in *Willy Wonka and the Chocolate Factory* when it was brought to life onscreen. Unfortunately, the adaptation of his own book didn't sail as smoothly as he'd hoped.

In the early stages of production, tension grew between Dahl and the filmmakers, and their creative differences threatened the project. His adaptation was a straightforward and linear translation of the book, while the filmmakers felt that more dynamic elements were needed to carry the story on the screen. Dahl, a purist, wasn't at all enthusiastic or receptive to ideas that shifted the story from his original version. In the end, Dahl's story underwent many significant changes, especially to the basic character elements and dialogue; there were also some very memorable additions.

David Seltzer, a talented young writer who, up to that point, had primarily worked with Wolper on documentary films, was brought in to develop and add texture to Dahl's screenplay (Seltzer later noted that it had consisted of only about fourteen pages). Seltzer would not receive an onscreen credit, but his arrangement with Wolper included a handshake deal that Wolper would produce his first independent screenplay (he later came through on that promise). Seltzer was flown to Munich and, with production in progress, he began polishing Dahl's already glistening story.

From Script to Screen

Not only did he have to adapt to using a German typewriter, he also had to write the dialogue that led into and out of the musical numbers—no easy undertaking for even the most seasoned of writers. Seltzer quickly identified an important missing ingredient: a villain, who would increase the suspense. In the book, there were rival candy makers, one of whom—Slugworth—was transformed by Seltzer into a more villainous and central character.

Seltzer proved to be an excellent choice to develop the smart and witty flavorings of Dahl's source material. He later generously said that he was simply following the lines of a really brilliant writer. Despite the complicated nature of their collaboration, Seltzer's skillful alterations were accomplished whilst maintaining the inventive charm of Dahl's original tale.

Although he didn't receive any onscreen credit for his writing contributions and re-crafting Dahl's original screenplay, David Seltzer was the wizard behind the curtain to which the film owes much of its success. His love and fluency for classic literature helped immortalize many of Willy Wonka's unforgettable lines in the film. He had never written a screenplay and the complexity of writing dialog around the musical numbers proved challenging. During a later interview when asked why he felt that the film had such cultural resonance, he commented while noting that the backgrounds of Wolper and Stuart were primarily in documentary rather than feature films: "We were really a bunch of amateurs flying by the seat of our pants and I think the film reflects that...It has that kind of energy. It's not the function of sitting down and intellectualizing...It's the function of cardboard...Scotch tape...let's put on a show. It's not the result of a ton of money...I think that's the flavor of what makes the movie so vital..." These ingredients created a magic formula that gave the film a heart.

This is one of my personal snapshots of the S.S. Wonkatania taken inside the massive Chocolate Room soundstage. Seen in the distance examining the vessel is the creative genius Harper Goff who designed all of the innovative sets for *Willy Wonka*. During shooting breaks I often ate lunch sitting next to the chocolate river while listening to the playback recording of "Pure Imagination." I enjoyed the tranquil setting and the opportunity for a quiet moment between takes.

The S.S. Wonkatania

THE S.S. WONKATANIA, a magical riverboat piloted by a crew of Oompa Loompas, was to Willy Wonka what Chitty Chitty Bang Bang was to Caractacus Potts: a magical sea vessel that could navigate imaginary places. The script indicated that our characters were to be filled with "exclamations of wonder, delight and excitement" when the boat is first spotted emerging from a dark tunnel that flowed into the chocolate river. While I had peeked into the Chocolate Room and had a fair knowledge of what to expect when we finally made our grand entrance, I hadn't seen the Wonkatania, and this proved to be a splendid and fun surprise.

The Wonkatania scene was an important transition from the Chocolate Room to another elaborate setting within the chocolate factory, and its filming was complicated by a variety of intertwining effects, which required transferring the vessel between three different soundstage locations.

A track system akin to that used by the Pirates of the Caribbean ride at Disneyland was laid into the foundation of the river, which was then filled with approximately 150,000 gallons of water and an improvised mixture of chemicals and conditioners. Cable pulleys were used to tow the vessel along the track system; and although I have no proof, I was led to believe that the Oompa Loompa who piloted the vessel actually believed that he was genuinely steering the boat.

Among Seltzer's signature contributions to the film were the clever and charming quotations, often borrowed from classic literature that he wove into Gene's dialogue. His fluency in these works translated into the elegance of the final script. Gene's quote from John Masefield's *Sea Fever*, "All I ask is a tall ship and a star to sail her by," along with many other graceful passages in a variety of languages, enhanced his character's sophistication without dampening his clever charm. Spotting the origins of these quotes has fascinated many Wonka fans and I think has helped in the longevity of the film's popularity.

Filming the Wonkatania scenes was extremely complex, due in part to the fact that each take required the boat to be manually "reset" to its starting point. When these scenes were completed, the Wonkatania was moved to another soundstage for the scenes requiring rear projection, and then finally to a third stage for the Inventing Room arrival segment.

The S.S. Wonkatania

Mounting friction among the cast and crew also complicated the process, and it was captured on a few frames of the final cut. Denise hated having to pick her nose onscreen, as it wasn't ladylike and was also a turn-off to Peter. Her lack of enthusiasm translated into having to do multiple takes, and each time, the boat had to be reset to its starting position. There was also tension between Peter and I during these scenes, due largely to my rivalry with Denise. We had a quarrel of sorts during filming. I can't remember exactly what Peter said to me, but it was apparently something I didn't like. Almost instantaneously, I snapped back with a smart-aleck remark that I thought was quite clever. A frequently reproduced cast photo shows all of us looking out to the river. In the photo, Peter is looking toward the camera rather wistfully and I'm looking down at my toes with a smug smile. I remember vividly that at the moment this photo was taken, I was feeling quite pleased with myself about my witty comeback to his remark.

By this point, Peter and I were no longer speaking to one another, and when we were invited by Gene to board the boat ("*Mesdames et messieurs, maintenant nous allons faire grand petit voyage par bateau. Voulez-vous entrer le Wonkatania?*" or "Ladies and gentlemen, now we are going for a great little boat trip. Do you want to come on the Wonkatania?"), I embarked with zest and then sat looking disinterestedly and pointedly away from Peter. There are frames within this scene in which Peter looks at me and I deliberately look away without making eye contact. That moment remains trapped in time for all to see. Of course, my annoyance passed quickly, and it wasn't long before I was back pursuing his attention.

When filming wrapped on the Chocolate Room scenes, the river was drained and the Wonkatania was transported to another soundstage. Stagehands began dismantling the stadium set and making way for the next film production, Bob Fosse's *Cabaret*, and the magical Chocolate Room began its transformation from a tangible place to images on film. There was a deep sense of loss as the enchanted landscape withered, reverting to a plain open soundstage.

Opposite: The scenes filmed in S.S. Wonkatania were accomplished on three separate soundstages, and proved to be some of the longest and most exhausting scenes to capture on film.

Once the Wonkatania was in place on the new set, it was elevated onto a large scaffold frame about twenty feet in the air. The only way up to the boat was by ladder. Once seated on this raised platform, we were stranded, unable to even use the restroom for long stretches during filming. It was during this period that I pleaded the most with Roy to perform his rendition of "Now, you've heard of Hiawatha?" again and again and again. We were trapped on this boat for hours together, and that generous and gracious man kept me amused during the long idle periods.

The stage backdrop was a theater-size projection screen where unsettling psychedelic images flashed in rapid succession, giving the impression that the Wonkatania was traveling through mind-twisting passages. While some of the dark imagery—gruesome pictures of a chicken being slaughtered, reptiles, and other creatures—made it into the final film print, much darker images, including one of a large-bore needle being injected into an arm, were never used. A portrait of Slugworth flashed by, very 1940s film noir, along with many other dark themes captured in our own expressions. Stagehands shook the scaffolding to give the illusion of motion, and large mounted light systems helped illuminate the cast members.

"Round the world and home again, that's the sailor's way!" Gene commenced this scene by quoting from William Allingham's *Homeward Bound*, and his performance was so convincing that some of us actually became a little fearful during the segment. It is not one of my more happy memories of the production, due in part to the working conditions. Imagine having to see those disturbing images for hours on end. It was not a comfortable process, to say the least.

The Wonkatania's arrival at the exterior entrance of the Inventing Room took place on a completely different soundstage. Although simple in design onscreen, the exterior was an elaborate set, with a shallow-water section for the mooring of the Wonkatania. Our "ship" had to be stabilized so that we could disembark in a natural manner. Gene's primary dialogue in this scene was delivered in German, and it required numerous takes before he was able to capture the quintessence of his invitation. Translated into English, what he said was: "My friends, please give me your attention. You have now come to the most interesting and, at the same time, the most secret room of my entire factory. Ladies and Gentlemen... the Inventing Room..."

The man of sweet wonder,
magic and mystery

The Broken Shoe (A Not-So-Cinderella Tale)

IN HOLLYWOOD, as well as in other film studios worldwide, modern filmmaking creates a grand symphony from tiny notes, small strokes meticulously woven into a flowing masterpiece. During what is often a disjointed and repetitive process, it is difficult to develop a sense of a film's totality, and *Willy Wonka and the Chocolate Factory* was no exception. Despite the shooting format, which worked to capture the storyline as written to script, events occasionally forced us to film out of sequence. For example, the case of the broken shoe.

We had completed filming the entrance segment of the Inventing Room and were scheduled to film the next scene when, mysteriously, Denise broke one of her buckle-style shoes, which were continuity throughout the film. The shoe was damaged to such extent that it couldn't be repaired by the prop crew, or even by a local cobbler. The wardrobe for Denise's character, Violet Beauregarde, had been assembled in New York, and the only solution was to order another pair from the fashionable boutique where they had originally been purchased. This required some creative schedule-shifting and ultimately, the Goose Room scene was shot next and out of sequence.

I Want it Now!

For decades, I have been a little suspicious of the circumstances surrounding this mishap. Denise's sister, who was also her chaperone, seemed to have an interest in one of the hotel employees, and I couldn't help but wonder if perhaps it had been engineered to buy a little more time in Germany. Violet Beauregarde was to meet her end in the final segment of the Inventing Room, which would, in turn, end her tenure in the production. I'll never know for certain and I don't have anything to support this theory, but I've always remained just a little skeptical about the timing. I also envied Denise—she would have a lengthy break, giving her time to tour Munich. The production schedule was rigorous and there was very little time to get away for a few hours, much less entire days. This schedule change also meant that I would now need to be prepared to perform my choreographed number sooner than I had planned. I was tired before I started!

Coming of Age

BY THIS STAGE OF THE PRODUCTION, I had been in Munich for well over a month, and the strain of missing my family was clearly evident in some of the letters I sent my mother. It would be several weeks before I could return to the modest but heartwarming comforts of English life.

My mother loved Karen Carpenter's touching "Close to You," and it seemed to be playing every time I turned on a radio, as was the Beatles "Ticket to Ride" reminding me that my ticket home was still away off. It felt as though Peter, Paul and Mary's performance of John Denver's "Leaving on a Jet Plane," was taunting me. These songs dominated the airwaves, sad reminders of home and the people I missed so much. So when I learned that my mother and sister Lynn would be coming to Munich to help me celebrate my thirteenth birthday, I was thrilled beyond words.

Even with my income added to the family budget, money was still tight. The majority of my earnings had to be saved to pay my school fees. My mother couldn't afford to travel by air; instead, she and Lynn made an exhausting journey by ferry and train. The trip started on a ferry across the English Channel and continued via a complex rail route through the Netherlands

and into Germany. My mother also brought with her a very, very special cargo, an extraordinary birthday cake from a bakery in Guildford, made to resemble the *Charlie and Chocolate Factory* book. She carried it all the way and by the time they arrived, both were completely exhausted. I was so excited and pleaded with them to come downstairs to sample the snails and frog legs—in retrospect, I doubt this was what they wanted after their arduous journey.

My mother posing in front of the Schloss Hotel.

My mother couldn't afford to miss much work, so their visit was limited to a short weekend stay. I treasured this special time together. We took in the sights around Munich on the tramway, watching in astonishment as the waltzing wooden figures emerged from the famous town hall clock, as they did every hour. We also enjoyed shopping, and one of my treasured gifts was a native Bavarian dress that mother insisted I wear to dinner on the evening of my birthday which would be the day after she left. We then retreated to the hotel and enjoyed long walks along the river, catching up on news from home.

Since my mother wouldn't be able to stay for my actual birthday, we celebrated a few days early in the hotel's restaurant, along with Peter and his mother. It was just lovely having my family be around and being able to introduce them to everyone. We cried with laughter as we shared birthday cake and drank soda to our hearts' content, but it ended all too soon.

My mother and sister's departure the following evening is a painful memory, one that has never left me. The afternoon before they left, we enjoyed quiet time in my hotel room, talking over tea as my mother carefully ironed

A photo series of my mother, sister Lynn, Peter and me on my 13th birthday at the Schloss Hotel in Germany. In October of 1970, my mother and sister traveled to Munich to be with me. As my mother couldn't afford airline tickets, both she and Lynn made the exhausting journey by ferry and train. She carried with her a very special birthday cake that she brought from a bakery in Guildford, made to resemble the *Charlie and the Chocolate Factory* book. To think that my mother carried that all the way from England!

my new dress. It was heart wrenching as we stood solemnly at the tram stop, hugging each other and saying our last goodbyes. Like something out of a movie, I stood waving as the tram slowly pulled from the stop, fading from sight under the darkening sky. It was a terribly lonely walk back to the hotel without them. After so many years, this memory still conjures up tears whenever I think about it.

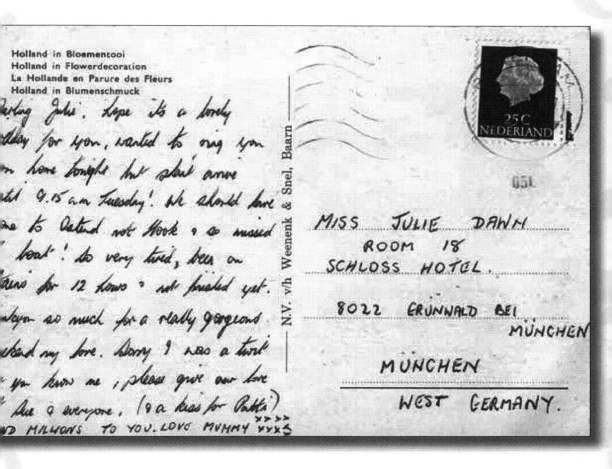

DEAR VERUCA SALT —
To THE MOST TALENTED
MOST CHARMING
MOST ATTRACTIVE
AND
MOST SPOILED AND ROTTEN
KID IN THE WHOLE WORLD!

HAPPY BIRTHDAY

STAN & HEL

Gooses.... Geeses... Filming the Goose Room scene with my endearing on-screen father Roy Kinnear as Henry Salt. Kinnear was a brilliant and acclaimed actor popular in both British and American productions. Roy treated me as if I were his own daughter during filming. The shooting schedule on this date was especially grueling with a record thirty-six takes required for one particular sequence and it also happened to be my thirteenth birthday. As his gift to me, Gene Wilder hired a color stills photographer to capture my big scene. The photos taken that day remain some of my most treasured and precious keepsakes from the production, and a fabulous record of my thirteenth birthday.

The Goose Room

THE ACTUAL DAY of my thirteenth birthday turned out to be very special, and remains my most memorable experience during the filming of *Willy Wonka*. When I arrived at the studio on Monday morning, Paris passed me with a big smile and wished me a happy birthday, which I thought was very sweet, as I hadn't expected anyone to even know. We began filming the initial segments of the Goose Room, which during these particular takes, comprised mostly of the entrance and early dialog. During the afternoon, I was asked to wait in the makeup suite in another part of the studio lot whilst the crew put the finishing touches to the set. As I waited there with Denise, suddenly the door flew open and Jack Row announced "God damn it Julie where have you been? Mel is going mad." I didn't need to be told twice. In absolute panic, I ran as fast as I could down the long dark corridor back to the set. The Goose Room was pitch black, but as my eyes adjusted, I realized the entire crew and cast were standing around a birthday cake, made especially for me lit with thirteen candles. We all enjoyed the cake for roughly five minutes, when Mel's benevolence ended, and he announced it was time to "get back to work!"

I Want it Now!

Gene Wilder gave me a priceless gift: He had hired a professional color photographer to capture the filming of my musical number that day and to record my entry into teenage-hood. His gift has lasted for nearly forty years and allows me to revisit those memories time and time again. The cast and crew gave me a special hand-drawn card with personal notes, which I still treasure. When we wrapped filming, we headed back to the Schloss, and I retired to my room, still buzzing, but also a little flat as it was my first birthday without my mother.

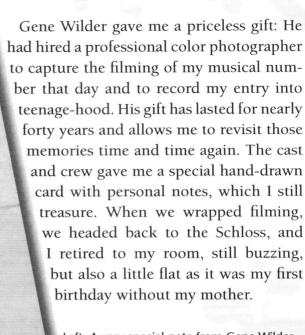

Left: A very special note from Gene Wilder on my thirteenth birthday. All of us absolutely adored Gene and my memory of this special day remains very dear.

Opposite and this page: These set photos were taken while rehearsing my scenes with Direc-tor Mel Stuart and Choreographer Howard Jeffrey. The Goose Room scenes were filmed on my thirteenth birthday, October 26, 1970. Note Mel's clutched fists urging me to be as revolting and mean as I could be. Also of note is Arthur Ibbetson behind me checking the scene lighting.

Right: Denise and me at my birthday party at the Schloss Hotel, wearing my Bavarian dress that my mother pressed so neatly for me and also the gift necklace given to me by Roy and his wife Carmel.

Below: One of the Oompa Loompa actors with American school tutor Judy Collins and Assistant Director Wolfgang Glattes. Following *Willy Wonka* Glattes remained at the Bavarian Film Studios to work with Bob Fosse on *Cabaret,* and later collaborated again with Fosse in the United States in the motion picture *All That Jazz.*

One of the first orders of the evening was to try on my new Bavarian dress. Denise came in and we both lay on the bed and were reading our favorite comics when my mother called to wish me a happy birthday. She seemed upset to hear that I was lying on the bed in my dress and getting it wrinkled. I couldn't understand why it bothered her so, and thought she was just exhausted from her long journey back home. After we said our goodbyes, my chaperone announced that it was time to head downstairs for dinner. I was tired from the long day and asked if we could just stay in our room for the night, but Sue was insistent that we go downstairs and have a proper meal. I gave in grudgingly...Little did I know that another surprise awaited.

Sue and I were led to a different room, where to my amazement almost everyone from the studio had come to attend my surprise party. I shared this with Peter whose birthday was to be a week later. This had all been arranged by Mel, and was the reason my mother had been so insistent about keeping my dress neatly pressed. She had known about the surprise party all along. I was showered with so many precious gifts. Jack Albertson gave me a miniature grandfather clock with beautifully hand-painted Austrian flowers. Roy Kinnear and his wife gave me my very first manicure set, in a beautiful burgundy leather case. They also gave me a gypsy-style necklace with layers of medallion pieces that I cherished and wore for many years. Denise gave me a pretty gold pendant with my astrological sign and birthday engraved on the back. Peter and the others also gave me gifts that I absolutely cherished. It was an enchanted evening, and I remember being so elated that everyone had made such an effort to help Peter and me celebrate our birthdays.

The remaining Goose Room scenes were shot over a period of several days. The complex choreography was accomplished through a multiplicity of takes. The scene in which my character shoves a cart into a tower of boxes became a personal record for the highest number of takes for a single shot, a record that has lasted the duration of my film career. It required thirty-six takes to get the images seen in the final film version. With each take, the boxes, along with the positions of the ribbons, were reset to maintain continuity. When the cart struck the boxes, they tumbled in an orderly manner with the help of bursts of compressed air. The geese were spliced in during postproduction, using projection screens against the original film print. Due to the limitations of the special-effect capabilities of this era, the script had been modified from Dahl's original story, which featured trained squirrels selecting walnuts, to geese that laid golden chocolate eggs. It was a clever transformation that worked perfectly on film. As I sang along to my prerecorded track, fellow cast members had to stand on their marks for five full days while I ranted and raged around the set in pure Veruca style. But I loved every minute, and my memories of the time are priceless.

In the grandest of finales, my character met her demise as she belted the last and sustaining notes of her musical anthem: "Don't care how...I want it NOWWWWWWWW!" I was more concerned as a teenage girl by the fact

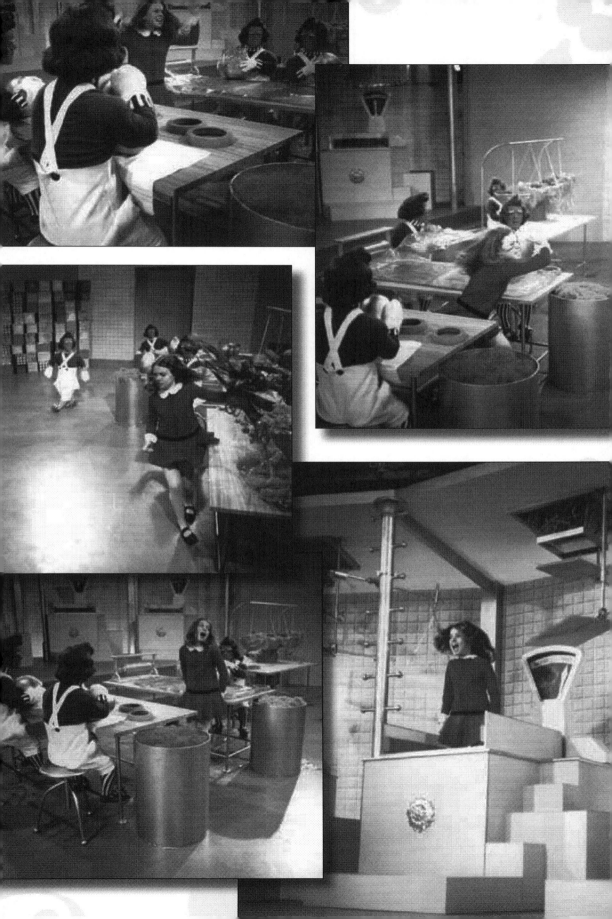

Dear Mummy, Lyn Nanny and Carol,
We have hired a car for the weekend
and we have been to loads of nice
places. We went to Lindhoss castle
Saturday Afternoon. I took some nice
snaps. There is a gold fountain there
which comes up every ten mins
by natural pressure. It was so high
I couldn't get it all in the photo.
We went on to Austria and stayed
in hotel in the mountains for the
night. There's about 6ft of snow in
parts. We have been right up in
the mountains today. I'm writing
this letter in Italy I'm really
getting around We have been over
the Brenner pass and the Fen Pass
Missing you all and longing to come
home All my love
X

Mrs P. S. Cole.

99, Bushy Hill Drive

Merrow

Guildford Surrey

ENGLAND

that when the egg chute's trap door was released, Bill Roe, the eldest son of the assistant director, Jack, was waiting below. Bill had been hired to test the trap door and made several runs to be sure that it functioned properly when fully weighted. At the base of the chute, Bill was instructed to catch me and prevent me from bouncing back up. A mattress was also positioned along with cardboard boxes to help break my fall, but it wasn't the fall that weighed so heavily on my mind. Bill was about sixteen and I thought he was cool, but not so cool that I wanted him to get an eyeful of me from below. To make matters even worse, another stagehand (or rather, another set of prying eyes) was also in the chute, peering

During one of our free weekends, Sue and I rented a car and drove into Austria. This photo was taken somewhere along the Brenner Pass (a mountain pass through the Alps) along the border between Italy and Austria.

up. All I could think about was that they were going to get a really good view up my dress and full view of my underwear. When it came time to film my finale, I made sure it was accomplished in one take and one take only. The shot itself was tricky: I needed to stand perfectly balanced and in the absolute center of the trap door, in order to avoid toppling either forward or backward and hitting my head. I also had to discipline myself not to put my arms out to break my fall, since that could also result in a serious injury.

While the Goose Room sequences were shot over a period of about five days, the sequence that involved me scaling up to the Eggdicator and falling into the chute was accomplished in a single take. To this day, I have no idea what they could see from below. When I emerged onto the forward set, I was met with applause by the entire cast and crew.

Opposite: It would seem fitting that during one of our production breaks, several crew, cast and their family members would travel to see Baron Bomburst's castle (which actually was the very historic Neuschwanstein Castle, located in Bavaria, Germany) from the classic 1968 film *Chitty Chitty Bang Bang*.

Leonard Stone "Square Deal Sam" standing along the perimeter wall of the 19th-century palace. A Tony-Award winner for his Broadway role in *Leonard* was a veteran actor in popular film and television programs such as *Mission Impossible, Dragnet, Dr. Kildare, Gunsmoke* and *Perry Mason.*

One of the few photos of my chaperone Sue Breen while touring the Neuschwanstein Castle.

Above and right: Sightseeing photos taken during a weekend outing with Roy and his wife Carmel Cryan at the Nymphenburg Palace in Munich.

The Goose Room

Roy finished the Goose Room scene, performing a funny bit of dialog with Gene, paired with a few ad-libbed comedy gestures. His closing moments were some of the most memorable as he performed a little trip when he landed on the chute's rim and then plunged in headfirst. He was a somewhat portly man, but light on his feet, and he put his heart and soul into that last bit. Entertaining people meant a great deal to Roy. He was such a wonderful man.

My first experience of "trick or treating" dressed in a Dutch national costume, October 1970 with American School Tutor Judy Collins, Paris and Bobby Roe. The gentleman (left) was visiting the set on this particular day, but his name and role are unknown.

Get on your cue—and I mean now! In the Director's seat while filming on the set of the Inventing Room. Visible in the background is Gene Wilder talking with the late Producer Stan Margulies and on the left Camera Operator Paul Wilson. Director Mel Stuart can also been seen in the background. Paul was brought to the production after collaborating with Arthur F. Ibbetson whose work together received an Academy Award nomination for best cinematography in *Anne of a Thousand Days* in 1969. The two had met while shooting a made for Television program *A Story of David* in 1960, and collaborated on eleven major productions before joining forces to film *Willy Wonka*. Additionally, Paul had worked on a variety of other classic motion pictures including the Beatles' *Hard Days Night*, *Help!*, *Moby Dick*, and *The Dirty Dozen*.

The Inventing Room

AT THE VERY HEART of Dahl's tale was the top-secret place where Willy Wonka formulated the ingredients of his most ingenious confectionary delights. The Inventing Room was described in the script as resembling a "witch's kitchen," with pots boiling, kettles hissing, and pans sizzling, and the finished set was simply marvelous. With Denise outfitted in her new shoes delivered fresh from New York, we began shooting what would be her final scenes in the film. Once more, in order to capture our spontaneous reactions, this set had also remained off-limits to us kids. It was great fun to explore, the nooks and crannies of this Wonka style adventure playground. Some of the quirkiest contraptions were hidden under cloth, their wondrous cogs and mechanisms concealed. Between takes, we snuck peeks under the covering at the marvelous machinery Harper Goff had designed with fellow engineers. To build the set, the designers had scoured Munich, searching for metal parts that, when creatively assembled, would be realistic parts of Wonka's creative utopia. I enjoyed watching the boxing gloves pumping up and down, the whimsical machinery hammering and squashing, and the different colors painted on the great gum machine. Gene was in truest form of character as he introduced his most astonishing inventions to us.

There were a variety of improvised sequences throughout. In one, an Oompa Loompa was originally intended to vigorously pedal the bicycle attached to a mixing contraption. However, on the day of production, it was discovered that none of them were tall enough to reach the pedals. So it was decided that Gene would pedal and sing verses from Shakespeare's comedy, *As You Like It*:

In springtime, the only pretty ring time
Birds sing, hey ding
A-ding, a-ding
Sweet lovers love the spring…

All of the cast members loved exploring the gadgetry while filming on the set of the Inventing Room.

The Inventing Room

The song came to a sudden halt when Paris's Mike Teevee sampled the exploding candy. Paris was quite excited about actually performing a stunt on-camera. The explosion triggered a spring-loaded retraction mechanism that propelled Paris, wearing a wire harness, into a clanging pan rack. Smoke from a tube along his cheek provided the illusion of residual smoke as he exhaled.

The Inventing Room scenes were filmed over the course of several weeks, and Paris was always looking for ways to amuse himself between takes. One of the most interesting set props, the great gum machine, utilized live wasps as stand-ins for the honey bees that naturally sweetened the gum Denise's character was soon to sample.

On a Monday morning, following an extremely cold weekend, all the wasps were found dead from exposure. Once another colony had been procured, "someone" decided to lift the glass dome, thus releasing the wasps. We were instructed to evacuate the studio to avoid being stung. The stagehands futilely attempted to recapture the wasps and this created a significant delay in filming. Paris has never admitted it, but I would just like to

Gene showing Jack, Peter and me Wonka's revolutionary, non-pollutionary mechanical wonder.

point out that he was the only one to be stung. Unluckily for him it was on his face and once again filming was halted. Mel was not in the best of moods and when filming reconvened the camera had to be repositioned to shoot Paris's good side. All these years later, Paris has yet to come clean about this.

Art Director Harper Goff showing off his magical confectionary machinery to Peter and Jack on the Inventing Room soundstage. I so enjoyed these fantastical sets with all of Goff's imaginative contraptions.

Despite the intensive shooting schedule, we enjoyed filming these scenes in such an eccentric environment. The Everlasting Gobstopper was in itself a revered and central figure of the story. Its secret ingredients were feverishly sought by rival confectioner Arthur Slugworth, and for the children who loved the story of *Charlie and the Chocolate Factory*, it was the grandest of grand, a symbol of sweet perfection, the baron of all candies.

At this stage in the production and after so many weeks filming, we had reached the point where we all felt at ease about offering ideas to enhance our characters when it seemed appropriate. One gesture earned me a close-up when Gene gives his commentary: "I can only give them to you if you solemnly swear to keep them for yourselves and never show them to another living soul as long as you all shall live. Agreed?"

My character, Veruca, can clearly be seen crossing her fingers behind her back. During one of the first takes, Mel halted the production to ask what I was doing, and once I explained, he liked the idea so much that he had me do it each take. When these scenes were finally completed to Mel's standards, we were rushed to the classroom for our required studies. As I got settled, I realized that cupped tightly in my hand was my Everlasting Gobstopper, which I had absentmindedly removed from the set. It was protocol for the prop master to retrieve all of the props from each actor, but we rushed off so quickly that there hadn't been time. My Everlasting Gobstopper became an everlasting souvenir. Many years later, I learned that I was the only naughty one who had kept their Gobstopper.

A rare photo of me doing homework during a production break. During the entire shooting schedule we were required to maintain our standard academic workload. During daily shooting breaks, we were rushed to our classrooms to complete the required daily three hours of schooling.

"Violet, You're Turning Violet, Violet!"

WONKA'S GOLDEN TICKET

THE FINALE for Denise's defiant character, Violet, was shot in several segments and involved numerous uncomfortable costume transitions. In her final scene, Violet was to stray and sample a chewing gum enhanced with the savory flavors of a three-course meal. We were to watch as she described each entrée and then witness her transformation into a blueberry during the dessert phase. At the beginning of her transition, simple blue flood lamps and makeup were used. In the next sequence, when Violet was to begin expanding, air bladders that could be remotely inflated were stitched inside her costume, which had elastic seams to allow the material to stretch. The final costume incorporated two large Styrofoam ball-shaped sections for which Denise had to be specially fitted. This costume took an incredible amount of time to set up and had to be applied and fitted on her in sections.

Once in costume, Denise had to remain in character for several hours. To minimize her discomfort and reduce pressure on any single part of her body, Denise was assigned an assistant whose sole responsibility was to turn her in different directions at specific intervals. I really felt sorry for her, as the costume was visibly uncomfortable and confining. During the Oompa

129

Loompa number, the actors had difficulty rolling Denise around as originally choreographed. It was a tight fit through the door section, and rolling her proved most challenging for this team of actors; on occasion they accidentally struck her head on the doorway's metal molding. The Oompa Loompas tried hard to synchronize their movements, but since there was no easy method to remain on mark during the musical number, they simply did their best to roll her without injuring her. The final costume was nearly as round as they were tall, and logistically, it was a very difficult scene to execute.

Denise had long, flowing, auburn hair, and, depending on where they cut in the scene, there were several occasions where her hair ended up tangled

Of all the child actors, Denise's character (Violet Beauregarde) had the most difficult wardrobe transition. While Michael was forced to wear wet clothing for hours on end, Denise was sandwiched between two large Styrofoam circular inserts to simulate her juice filling expansion into a blueberry, all the while wearing thick blue facial makeup. She was so tightly encased in this costume that going to the bathroom was an impossible feat, as removal from this special outfit was a once a day operation only. I felt very sorry for her as the Oompa Loompas rolled and steered her around the set, to quote her own words, she doubted whether they had Oompa Loompa driving licenses.

around her face, which was clearly uncomfortable. Between takes, I tried to brush it away from her face, which she seemed to appreciate. Denise later recalled that when we stopped filming for lunch, she was left there for almost an hour since it wasn't possible to remove her costume for a short period.

For me, it was very sad when Denise's scenes finally wrapped filming. We had become as close as sisters, and really had fun together, hanging out on weekends and evenings in our hotel rooms. But there were no long good-byes—when she completed her segments, she was immediately flown home to New York. (Denise had an odd experience when she returned to school. Still jet-lagged, she was sitting in class when her face started to turn blue again. Puzzled, she ran to the bathroom to look into a mirror and sure enough, her face had a bluish hue. As it turned out, the makeup had seeped deep into her pores, only to resurface again a few days later.) My scenes were also close to completion; there were only three scenes left to shoot. We promised to write each other often, and did so for quite a while, but over time, we lost touch. It was well over twenty-five years before we saw each other again.

Director Mel Stuart sharing a light moment between takes while filming the Wonkamobile scenes with Gene and Producer Stan Margulies.

Bubbles, bubbles everywhere, but not a drop to drink...Yet.

"Snozzberries? Who Ever Heard of a Snozzberry?"

WITH THE FILMING of all my major scenes inside the Chocolate Factory complete, I was able to have a free weekend without rehearsals, and took time to simply relax. Our next scene was a transitional one, set in the edible wallpaper corridor that led into the room where Wonka made his Fizzy Lifting Drinks. The fruit-patterned lickable wallpaper was one of my favorite scenes and was accomplished in a rather quick fashion, aside from a few uncomfortable aspects. In this scene, Willy Wonka invites us to sample the wallpaper:

WILLY WONKA: *Wait a minute. Must show you this. Lickable wallpaper for nursery walls. Lick an orange, it tastes like an orange. Lick a pineapple, it tastes like a pineapple. Go ahead, try it! Try some more... The strawberries taste like strawberries. The snozzberries taste like snozzberries!*
VERUCA: *Snozzberries? Who ever heard of a snozzberry?*

This has always been one of my favorite lines in the movie. It was dynamic on script and linguistically fun to deliver. Another subtle but crucial element was that this was the only point in the story where one of the child characters challenged Willy Wonka directly. Gene captured the moment in what I think is one of the most profound quotations, from Arthur O'Shaughnessy's *Ode*. His graceful retort to my snidely delivered comment: "We are the music-makers, and we are the dreamers of dreams…"

Gene then squeezed my cheeks, forcing me to reveal my candy-tinted tongue. The production staff used a powdery, chalky-tasting food coloring to create the red snozzberry residue, and I had to wash off my tongue at the finish of each take. It was a bit uncomfortable, but quite fun nonetheless. The wallpaper actually had a sugary jam on it, so there was some taste for cast members. This scene was fairly straightforward, and when we wrapped it, the Fizzy Lifting Drink Room—where Peter and Jack's characters sampled the gravity-defying (and forbidden) beverage—was our next segment.

The Fizzy Lifting Room stage was actually comprised of three different sections to replicate the vent stacks. This also proved to be a challenging scene since the soaps bubbles stung our eyes as they popped.

"Snozzberries? Who Ever Heard of a Snozzberry?"

The filming conditions on the Fizzy Lifting Drink Room set were some of the most uncomfortable. The set was outfitted with several machines that produced bubbles high in soap content, and when the bubbles burst, they made our eyes water. It was difficult to look natural and maintain a sense of wonderment while trying not to shed tears.

Peter and Jack were fitted with uncomfortable wire harnesses so they could "fly" into the air as the Fizzy Lifting Drinks took effect. The machines had metal spears, and during filming, Peter and Jack were raised over them in their harnesses. Peter later confided that being suspended by wires above the machines while doing somersaults and being jerked up and down by the stagehands controlling their ascent was extremely unnerving. I didn't spend much time on this set, as the scenes of Peter and Jack ascending didn't require us.

My original Wonka and Scrumdidilyumptious Bar props from the production. Note the wrapper on the Wonka bar is actually cardboard with a silver paint finish.

Finding My Golden Ticket

MY FINAL SCENES to be shot were actually my first to appear in the movie. Veruca Salt's opening scene was a critical introduction for my character; this was where the audience first met Veruca and the scene established her bratty persona. It was in Salt's Peanut Factory that Veruca's Golden Ticket was found, thanks to her wealthy father's unwavering quest to please her.

The Peanut Factory set was truly majestic—we were astounded by how realistic it was. Constructed fully to scale on one of the vast soundstages, it incorporated thousands of prop candy bars and discarded wrappers. The set designers used a mixture of rewrapped Hershey bars along with wooden bars—a high level of detail for this one scene. I remember being awestruck.

Pat Coombs was a beloved British comedienne well known for her work on television and radio, and I was a particularly big fan of hers. She was cast as my mother, Henrietta Salt, and I was excited to meet and share scenes with her.

My wardrobe also included something that was very special to me, a necklace that held a silver sixpence for good luck. My mother had given it to me

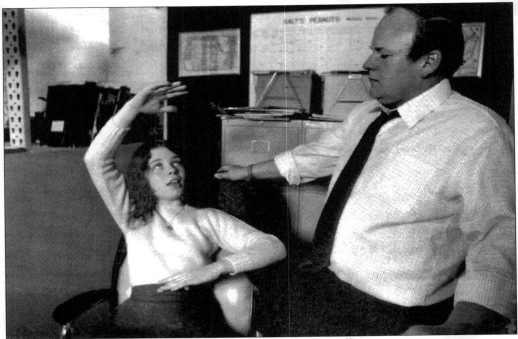

Roy and me filming our scene inside the Salt Peanut Factory office.

for my twelfth birthday, and had given an identical one to my sister Lynn on hers. It was a very special piece of jewelry, and both Mel and producer Stan Margulies eventually gave their approval for me to wear it on-screen. There was a debate about it, since they had also considered having me wear an expensive locket, but I pleaded and to my delight they agreed.

Another issue also embarrassingly provoked rather a lot of debate. When this scene was filmed, I was entering a growth phase and had started to develop in a certain area! This presented Mel and Stan with a dilemma. I was wearing a pale tight fitting sweater, and they stood scrutinizing me, discussing whether I would have to wear some kind of device known as "binders." I managed to talk them out of this humiliating requirement and was allowed to be all me onscreen.

Another intriguing piece of *Wonka* trivia: caring for split ends was an obsession for our hair stylist, Susi Krause. Her technique to remedy them involved slightly dampening and then twisting large hanks of hair into something resembling a rope. Then, using a candle, she carefully burned off the split ends. Since we filmed some segments out of sequence, in the scene where I find my Golden Ticket, my hair is considerably shorter than it was when we entered Wonka's factory gates.

The office scenes with Roy and Pat were intended to define how nasty Veruca could be, and I remember Mel pushing, pushing, and pushing me to be meaner. As I spun harder and harder in the chair, Mel challenged me to go to new depths to extract the meanest and most vile attitude I could conjure for Veruca. There were so many memorable elements to these scenes. I still vividly remember those lines—they were so much fun for a young actress!

"I wanted to be the first to find a Golden Ticket, Daddy…"
"All right, where is it? Why haven't they found it?"
"I want it now! What's the matter with those twerps down there?"
"Make 'em work nights."

The Salt Peanut Factory set was absolutely enormous. It spanned one entire massive Bavarian Studio soundstage, and the level of detail was simply staggering. Ironically, our first scenes were completed towards the end of the production schedule.

"They're not even trying. They don't want to find it. They're jealous of me."

"You promised, Daddy! You promised I'd have it the very first day!"

"I won't talk to you ever again. You're a rotten, mean father. You never give me anything I want. And I won't go to school 'til I have it."

At that moment, a young worker finds my ticket and is assisted by Slugworth to the stairwell so I could snatch it from her. I still remember the actress and how sweet I thought she was. As I recall, she was German but with a perfect English accent. I'm fairly certain her name was Steffie, and she made a lasting impression on me.

Up to this point, Günter Meisner (the odious Arthur Slugworth) and I had interacted very little, and as we entered the gates to Wonka's factory, I recall being suspicious of him. We never saw him off-set and I expect this was by design. Among other things, he had a scar—a highly realistic make-up effect—that enhanced his spine-chilling appearance. As we ascended the stairwell, he caressed my hand and whispered in such a creepy manner that I was sincerely frightened. Those whispers are the mystery that fans of the movie always beg me to reveal. So what were those words? Well… if Günter did intend a special message on the stairs that day, he took it with him to his grave. His whispers were just that: indiscernible murmurs. When we finally completed shooting, I discovered that Günter was a very nice man; he apologized for the dark demeanor he had assumed while in character, which he felt was the only way to provoke a genuine response from us. Well, it certainly worked with me.

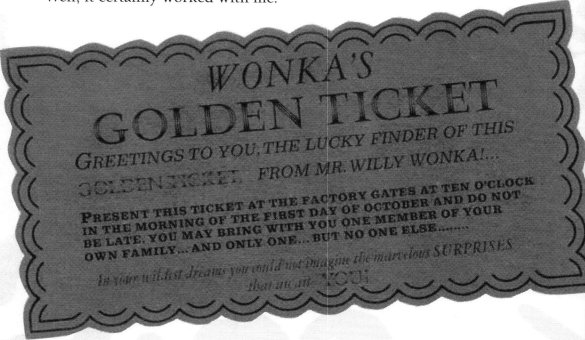

One of the most common questions posed by fans of the film, is what exactly did Arthur Slugworth whisper to you? Well...I'm not telling...Okay, just not here as it's exposed elsewhere in the book. But the character dialog is actually all revealed in this scene with Peter Ostrum and Günther Meisner. The character of Arthur Slugworth was not only sinister and frightening on film, but Günther Meisner did a good job off-camera staying in character all the time. To our surprise once we all wrapped our scenes together, we actually discovered that Günther, unlike Slugworth was extremely nice and amiable.

WOLPER PICTURES, LTD.

Bavaria Atelier GmbH
Postfach 900229
8 München 90, GERMANY
Tel. 64991
cable bavariaatelier munich

Julie Dawn Cole
99 Bushey Hill Drive
Guildford
Surrey

25 November 1970

Dear Julie:

You are gone - but not forgotten.

I just wanted to tell you again how much we enjoyed
having you with us. Your very professional approach
to your work, as well as your fine performance, made
our association a pleasure.

I hope you are now comfortably settled at home again
and at school. Best wishes from all of us for everything
good.

Sincerely,

Stan Margulies

SM:is

P. O. BOX 900 · BEVERLY HILLS, CALIFORNIA 90213 · (213) 277-2211 · CABLE CENTFOX LOS ANGELES

O N A COLD, overcast day in early November 1970, the filming of my segments were finally completed. On the day Sue
and I departed for home, we visited the studio one last time to
say goodbye. Many of the soundstages were already being torn
down and transformed into a 1930s Berlin stage set for Bob Fosse's *Cabaret*,
which later garnered eight Academy Awards. (In the "small world" category,
not only had Joel Grey been one of the top choices for the role of *Willy
Wonka* before Gene was cast, Fosse would later share the stage with Gene in
the endearing 1974 musical production of *The Little Prince*.)

Saying goodbye to Roy and the rest of the cast was difficult, as we had
grown very close over the weeks of production. When I arrived, the production crew were busy preparing for Paris's scene in the TV room. We had to
watch from a distance since we were not allowed to enter the set and dirty
the perfect white floor. Dodo Denney (who played Paris's mother and re-
ferred to him as *meine kleine maus*, German for "my little mouse" was one of
the first to greet us and to wish us goodbye. Gene, Jack, and Mel each gave
me a warm hug, and I struggled not to cry. But saying goodbye to Peter was
even more heart-wrenching.

I Want it Now!

My affection for Peter was deep, and it was a difficult parting. I remember such anguish when I knew the time had come to say goodbye. While we were too young for our relationship to be romantic, there was no question in my mind that I was saying goodbye to my very first love.

Above: The final scenes of the film. Peter later reminisced that during the latter stages of production, probably as the only child left, he would often have lunch with Gene. They would walk back to the soundstage and share a chocolate bar for dessert.

Opposite: The Wonka Vision set... This was the last set I visited prior to leaving Germany. Everyone not involved in the shooting was kept at a distance so as not to dirty the pristine white floor.

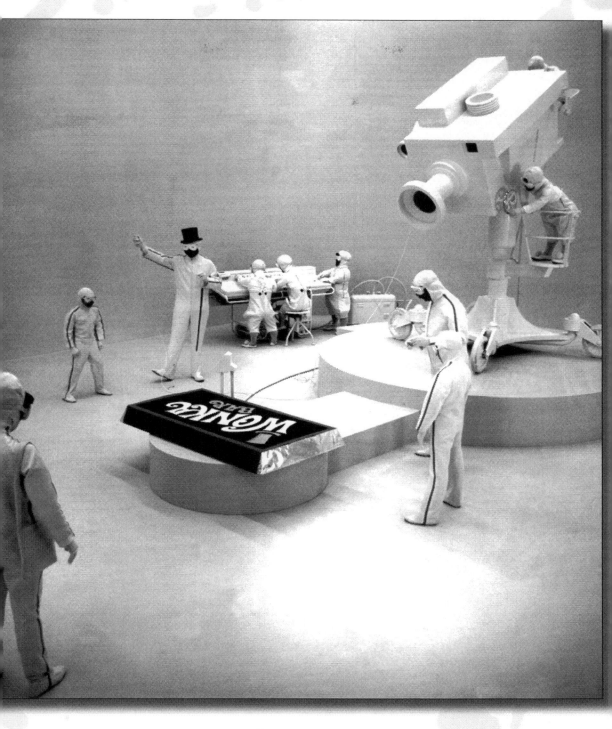

Home Again

ARRIVING AT HEATHROW, I greeted my mother and suggested that we hail a taxi to take us home. To which my mother quickly responded, "No, darling, we have to get the train." The days of studio cars, fancy dining and other luxuries were over. All that were left were my special memories, and I had many of those.

Back at home in our kitchen, I regaled my mother and sister with stories of my funny experiences—how I had to explain to the customs official why I was bringing a "Golden Egg" into Britain, fights with Denise over Peter, and the many privileges I had enjoyed each day. Things at home had not changed at all, and it was nice being there again with my mother, Lynn, and my dog, Lucy. I had missed them all so much. With little fanfare, I returned to school, traveling back and forth each day by train as I had done hundreds of times before and was reunited with my best school friend Lindy Sellars. Enjoying sleepovers once more, and sharing out my candy spoils with her that I had brought back from Germany. Just occasionally, I would take out my Everlasting Gobstopper, a nostalgic reminder of my special time with *Willy Wonka*.

During the following year, I secured my first television role as Arabella, the bratty girl next door in the popular British television series, *And Mother Makes Three*. One of my co-stars was my classmate, David Parfitt (who has since enjoyed a prolific career in film and television, including producing the Academy Award–winning films *The Madness of King George* and *Shakespeare in Love*).

The final production segments for *Willy Wonka and the Chocolate Factory* were completed on November 19, 1970, and it was officially released in London in July 1971. My excitement grew as the release date drew near. Throughout production, I had never been invited into the screening room to preview the dailies, and had no idea how everything would appear on film. Having to wait so many months was absolute torture.

Opposite: During the publicity phase of *Willy Wonka*, my sister Lynn and I were featured our local newspaper, the *Surrey Advertiser*, holding a golden egg from the film. I carried this memento all the way back from Germany, and explaining to the customs agent why I was carrying a golden egg still makes me laugh when I remember his perplexed expression.

It's Scrumdidilyumptious!

It's everybody's non-pollutionary anti-institutionary, pro-confectionery factory of fun!

DAVID L. WOLPER
presents

"WILLY WONKA & THE CHOCOLATE FACTORY"

starring

GENE WILDER   JACK ALBERTSON and introducing PETER OSTRUM as Charlie

ROY KINNEAR   DENISE NICKERSON   LEONARD STONE   JULIE DAWN COLE   PARIS THEMMEN   DODO DENNEY

Directed by **MEL STUART**   Produced by **STAN MARGULIES** and **DAVID L. WOLPER**   Screenplay by **ROALD DAHL**   Based on his book "Charlie and the Chocolate Factory"

Lyrics and Music **LESLIE BRICUSSE   ANTHONY NEWLEY**   Musical supervisor **WALTER SCHARF**   A PARAMOUNT PICTURE

G   ALL AGES ADMITTED   Color by TECHNICOLOR*   SOUNDTRACK ALBUM AVAILABLE ON PARAMOUNT RECORDS

The London Royal Premiere

IN LATE SPRING, while in London waiting for my train, my eyes were drawn to a poster prominently displayed inside the station. There he was: Gene as Willy Wonka in his "Pure Imagination" scene, arms spread wide. In bold letters, the whimsical tag line, "It's Scrumdidilyumptious!" arched across the top of the poster. And there I was, too, standing atop Gene's arm in a pose taken from my musical number. Seeing myself on a movie poster in a bustling metropolitan train station was pretty surreal, and when I arrived home, I was barely able to describe the experience to my mother and sister.

The film's official film release was marked by two galas, the first held at the Ziegfeld Theatre in New York, and the second, a royal premiere in London with Princess Margaret in attendance. I had hoped to see my fellow cast members at the premiere, but had not been invited to New York. I later heard that Gene, dressed as Willy Wonka, had served guests ice cream from the Wonkamobile, which they had on display at the opening.

Early in the planning stage, the London premiere was accompanied by some controversy. I learned that I was going to be asked to present the traditional bouquet of flowers to Princess Margaret and was absolutely thrilled.

151

The long formal dress that my mother purchased for me to wear at the premier. I was excited at the prospect of wearing my first long dress; imagine my sadness on hearing that this would not be appropriate for a matinee affair. Even though I wasn't able to wear it for the actual screening, I was determined to wear it at some point in the evening and made a quick change in the ladies room before going out to dinner with my family.

Roald Dahl would also be attending, along with several other members of show business. With this in mind, my mother took me shopping to find a picture-perfect dress. We scoured all of London until we came upon the most beautiful full-length yellow dress that I had ever laid eyes upon. I had never owned a full-length gown and was thrilled beyond words.

Then, on short notice, we were told there had been a change in plan. Since the movie was considered a children's film and was scheduled to be shown at 6:15 p.m., it was decided that it would be treated as a matinee-style afternoon event rather than an evening premier. This meant that my full length dress was inappropriate and my mother was forced to buy me another dress, with strict instructions that it was to be knee length and not long. We were also disappointed to learn that we would only be given two tickets; since we certainly couldn't leave out my sister and my grandmother, two more had to be purchased. Tickets for this event were going for an astronomical price, and somehow my mother had to find the money to pay for this.

The royal premiere itself was incredibly exciting, but balanced against the thrills were complicated logistical issues. I was to present the bouquet of flowers to Princess Margaret in the main theater lobby. However, royal protocol dictated that once the Princess had entered the main floor of the theater, no one would be permitted to enter behind her. My mother

Roald Dahl and me at the London Royal Premier of *Willy Wonka and the Chocolate Factory* in December of 1971.

My exciting evening at the London Royal Premier.

desperately wanted to see me present the bouquet, but if she did, she wouldn't be allowed into the theater to watch the film. After some pleading with members of the Princess's royal entourage, my mother was permitted to stay with me and then we would discreetly return to our seats. My mother later teased me, saying there weren't any petals left on the flowers, as I was shaking so nervously when I made the presentation.

Despite my anxiety, Princess Margaret was very gracious. I remember being confused about whether to curtsey first and then hand her the flowers, or vice-versa. Roald Dahl and his wife, Patricia Neal (an accomplished actress who had been in many classic motion pictures, including *Breakfast at Tiffany's*, *In Harm's Way*, and *The Subject Was Roses* to name only a few), were both in attendance and stood in the reception line alongside me. Roy and his wife were also there and, as always, he looked after me. Many other celebrities also attended, including British actor David Hemmings, an icon of the 1960s and an actor on whom I'd had a huge crush when I was younger. How thrilling it was to have him there!

As the princess made her way to her seat, we were quickly escorted to ours, which were located far back in row 'O', in a section not exactly considered prime seating. It was here that I experienced *Willy Wonka and the Chocolate Factory* for the very first time. Even decades later, it is difficult to describe the feelings I had upon seeing myself on the huge screen, but I do recall being extremely critical of my performance. After the final credits rolled, I sped into the restroom and changed into my beautiful full length yellow dress, determined to wear it at some point in this magical evening. The family and I went for dinner in London and what a treat that was. I

Presenting the bouquet of flowers to Princess Margaret. Also standing in the reception line are Roald Dahl and his wife Patricia Neal. The experience was incredibly surreal, especially considering my background. I was terribly nervous when meeting the Princess and forgot all Royal protocols for etiquette. Despite all this, she was very gracious and warm towards me and it was an experience that we talked about in our family circles for some time. However, my privileged status didn't even run as long as the reception line. Once the Princess made her exit, we were quickly ushered to our seats towards the rear of the theatre in row 'O' (Not exactly what I would consider prime seating). But it was from this seat, I watched *Willy Wonka and the Chocolate Factory* for the very first time.

had been to my first premier, been presented to Princess Margaret, and was wearing an evening gown.

The following morning, we began scouring the reviews, not all of which were terribly kind—one critic remarked that the movie was "fun, but not funny." It seemed that the dark characters didn't connect well with the adult audiences. *Willy Wonka* was an extreme departure from Disney-style children's films, and in the end, it never found a solid adult audience during its run in the theaters. The same was true in the United States, though

Denise also kept in-touch with fellow cast members following the production. A few years after *Willy Wonka*, she sent me this photo of her visiting Bobby and his younger brother Tim at their home in Los Angeles.

it did get some positive reviews. For example, critic Roger Ebert said that "*Willy Wonka and the Chocolate Factory* is probably the best film of its sort since the *Wizard of Oz*. It is everything that family movies usually claim to be but aren't: delightful, funny, scary, exciting, and, most of all, a genuine work of imagination."

On a few occasions, I saw the movie at matinees in the downtown cinema with friends and family. There was something profoundly odd about sitting in a dark theater, anonymous to the other movie-goers riveted by the film's action. Their laughter, gasps, and smiles gave me a sense of pride, but I also paid a price for playing an unsympathetic character. During one memorable day at the cinema, I got a shock. As images of Veruca filled the screen during her grand finale, the crowd broke into cheers when she went down the chute. I gasped in shock—I was a still a kid, and this experience was tough. In London, as I walked to the train station, I often passed the cinema as the movie-goers exited, and on occasion, I heard people whispering to one another, "I think that's her…" But after several weeks, the most sobering moment of all arrived: the posters disappeared from the train station. The dream was over.

Willy Wonka and the Chocolate Factory was released during an era when home video didn't exist. Films would occasionally show up on television, but the primary life of the film was within the magic walls of the cinema. The experiences I had while part of the *Willy Wonka* cast remained very special to me, but life went on. *Willy Wonka and the Chocolate Factory* was soon to find its audience in the hearts of children around the world. Its magic re-entered my life in a defining way decades later.

Willy Wonka tapped into some of the most creative musical forces known in filmmaking during that era. Over the course of his career, Leslie Bricusse was nominated for eight Academy Awards which included his shared nomination with Anthony Newly and Walter Scharf for Best Music, Scoring Adaptation and Original Song Score for *Willy Wonka and the Chocolate Factory*. Bricusse had already won an Academy Award for Best Original Song "Talk to the Animals" in *Doctor Dolittle*. Bricusse not only composed the musical elements to *Doctor Dolittle*, but also wrote the screenplay. Rob Newman's Uncle Lionel (who happened to be the brother of the great composer Alfred Newman to whom the scoring stage at 20th Century Fox is named after), conducted the orchestra for this epic film and later won his own Oscar for *Hello, Dolly*.

Angels

THOUGH I WAS CONTENT to return to my quiet life in Guildford, I often thought about my friendships with Peter and Denise as well as with the other cast members during my daily commutes to and from London. Life at Barbara Speake was a steady routine of acting and academics, and I continued to get jobs in both stage and television productions.

Producers for the *And Mother Makes Three* series decided to add more dimension to the plot and married off the Sally Harrison character (played by Wendy Craig), after which the series became *And Mother Makes Five*. Lucky for me, this added another season to my work schedule. Before turning sixteen, I appeared in a very enjoyable television project with Rex Harrison's granddaughter; she and I played school friends. Once again, the close-knit nature of the film world was evident. Rex Harrison, who had played in some of the greatest motion pictures of the 1950s and 60s, including *Cleopatra* and *My Fair Lady*, was cast as Doctor John Dolittle alongside Anthony Newley in the classic *Doctor Dolittle*. Newley's partner, Leslie Bricusse, had written the screenplay for *Dolittle* and the duo later wrote the music for *Willy*

The cast of the popular BBC television series *Angels* (L-R): Me, Lesley Dunlop, Clare Clifford, Fiona Fullerton, Erin Geraghty and Karan David.

Wonka and the Chocolate Factory. This was the last project I took before leaving school.

After leaving Barbara Speake in 1974, I decided that I should have a back-up plan. I considered "normal" occupations and narrowed my choice to copy typist—the prospect of steady work was essential if not appealing. I took work at a couple of dreary travel agencies, then later, a job at the Royal Automobile Club, filing insurance claims, which proved to be one of the most tedious occupations on the face of the earth.

During the summer, I auditioned for a part in a new television series, *Angels*, which had been created by the producer of a popular British program, *Z Cars*. *Angels* was to be to nursing what *Z Cars* had been to the police. I returned for my final audition on Christmas Eve, and was elated when I was notified that I had been selected for a part. *Angels* followed the lives of six young nurses at St. Angela's Hospital in London and became an

A tongue in cheek autograph for my mother on an official cast photo we used for fan requests. Note my halo over my first name!

To Mum
With love
Julie Dawn Cole

(official autograph)

incredibly popular series. My good-hearted character, Jo Longhurst, was a second-year nurse who continually found herself in some sort of trouble. Production began in February 1975, and the pilot episode aired on September 1 on BBC1.

Angels not only established me as a household name in British television, but also as an adult actress. By this time, *Willy Wonka* was completely forgotten, and this new series defined a new chapter in my life and a new persona for me. *Angels* proved to be an excellent creative platform as well, giving me an opportunity to work with a variety of well-known guest actors and actresses. I developed close and long-standing friendships with my co-stars and enjoyed the experience immensely.

In Britain, the television work that I'm perhaps best known for was my work on the popular primetime 1970's television medical-drama series *Angels*. I was cast as Jo Longhurst, a second year student nurse who's overly caring and good willed nature often landed her in trouble. Filming *Angels* was a wonderful experience and something I remain very proud to be a part of. Even now I often meet nurses who tell me that *Angels*, and sometimes even my own character, was their inspiration for their career in nursing careers. What greater privilege can there be? During the two years I worked on the series many talented artists passed through the doors of the fictitious St. Angela's Hospital.

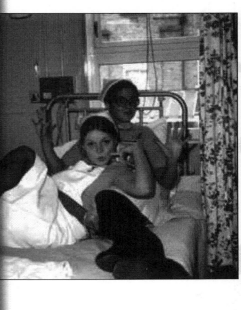

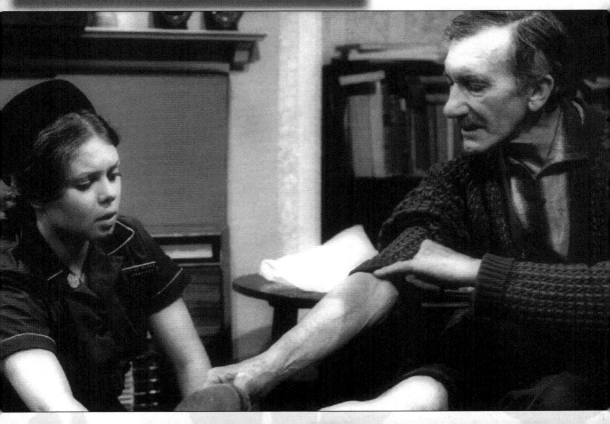

I Want it Now!

My family life during this period also changed. When she was nineteen, my sister Lynn married and left home. My mother secured a good job with Coutts Bank in London and together, she and I moved to Thornton Heath, a modest suburb of Surrey. We had reached a comfortable phase in our lives and were both quite content. Sometimes we spent evenings reading the fan mail that never seemed to stop pouring in

Above: A photograph of me in front of my home in Thornton Heath with my very first car (1975).

Below: Lucy, our loving family dog and me in 1976.

Above: Whether it be cage diving with great white sharks in South Africa or parachuting in Peterborough (as depicted here in 1976), I've always been one for adventure.

from fans of the *Angels* series and *Willy Wonka* had appeared to have been forgotten.

I had just turned eighteen, when I was invited to a celebrity soccer match to perform the kick-off. During the event, I met a musician named Peter Phipps. He was a young handsome drummer in a hugely popular British band of the 1970s, *The Glitter Band*. The two of us quickly became inseparable, and during scheduled production breaks from *Angels*, I followed Peter whilst he toured. I guess I was a "Rock Chick" and often found myself

Peter Phipps (seated left), drummer in the hugely popular British band of the 1970s, *The Glitter Band*. During the peak of their success, the band enjoyed numerous hits in the European and American pop charts.

Signing autographs for fans of the *Angels* series during a celebrity football event in 1975.

Peter and me in 1976. The two of us were inseparable until our split in 1979.

Below: Peter Phipps on the River Usk, South Wales (1976).

backstage at concerts with bands like the Who, Hot Chocolate, and Slade—it was a very exciting time.

The newfound success that both Peter and I enjoyed also brought with it newfound freedom. We bought a house together in Bromley, a small suburb of Kent, and I commuted to the studio, driving my small and very beaten-up little Mini back and forth to Birmingham, a hundred-mile trek each way. Work remained plentiful during this period. I continued getting jobs in both television and film, and occasionally was able to fit in some theater. The projects varied from small to major-budget productions and allowed me to work alongside some of the bigger stars at that time.

On holiday with Peter and my dog Lucy on a narrow boat (1976).

Poldark

I N LATE 1976, I left *Angels* after receiving and accepting an offer of a part in *Poldark*, a hugely popular costume drama series. During my Christmas break, and before filming started on the *Poldark* series, I also took the leading role in a Christmas theater production of the Frank Baum's *The Wizard of Oz*, which was performed at the historic York Theatre Royal. I was cast as Dorothy and my assistant stage manager was none other than Pierce Brosnan (who is, of course, now a little more well known). Pierce also held some smaller roles in the production, including one as an angry tree, one of the witch's soldiers, and a few others. My agent at the time was Felicity Larner, who came to see me in the production, and I introduced her to Pierce. He was straight out of drama school and she offered to represent him. Soon after, he won a part in the *Nancy Astor* television series which eventually took him to America. Had it not been for Felicity coming to see me in *The Wizard of Oz*, would Pierce still be brewing my tea? Okay, well, maybe that's going a little far, but things certainly may have been different had he not met my agent.

Production on *Poldark* began at the conclusion of *The Wizard of Oz*, and I was back to playing a nasty character, the promiscuous Rowella Warleggan.

I Want it Now!

The classic story of Dorothy in *The Wizard of Oz* remains one of the most cherished stories from my childhood. I was cast in the role of Dorothy in a theatre production in the city of York which ran Christmas of 1976. An unknown newcomer to acting named Pierce Brosnan was the assistant stage manager. Playing the dream role of Dorothy and getting to sing the classic "Over the Rainbow" every night remains a highlight of my career.

Poldark was based on the historical works of English novelist Winston Graham and revolved around Cornish squire Ross Poldark. When Ross returns to Cornwall after fighting in the American war of independence, he finds his estate in complete chaos, families bickering, and small-town politics raging. On occasion, he crosses swords with his rival and my character's cousin, George Warleggan. The story chronicled the hidden struggles, dramas, and societal conflicts these Cornish families faced in 1790s England, including some of the darker elements.

Initially, *Poldark* was a dream job for me. Although I couldn't relate to the loathsome Rowella, the chance to wear fantastic costumes and recreate the past was very enticing. I relished the chance to appear in a period drama particularly one of this caliber. Costume drama was something the BBC did exceptionally well. However, my relationship with one of the directors of the series Roger Tucker, was not to run smoothly.

The day before I was scheduled to travel to Cornwall, where all the exterior scenes were filmed, I received a bundle of thirteen scripts. This wasn't unusual, since the scripts often weren't completed until the last minute. I scanned them, looking quickly at my scenes, and was aghast when I found that my character would be appearing in a variety of topless and fully nude scenes. Putting it mildly, this was not what I had signed up for, and I was

On location in Cornwall during the filming of *Poldark* with me in period costume where I played an eighteenth century version of Veruca Salt; the promiscuous, manipulative and delightfully evil Rowella Warleggan.

flabbergasted. I immediately went to see my agents and told them how appalled I was. In the cold light of print, the scenes seemed to be very graphic for Sunday evening family television.

Roger Tucker, was not at all sympathetic to my plight. I had never been told, nor asked how I felt about the level of nudity that would be required. Roger had casually inferred at the casting, that there might be some nudity but it would be minor and not significant. I was only eighteen and felt bullied, manipulated and intimidated. I had a brief and heated exchange with Tucker. It was horribly unpleasant and only seemed to make matters worse. He offered no compromise—instead, he insulted me, saying, "You bloody actresses; you're all the same. . . . You'll say anything to get the part." He was implying that I had agreed to do the scenes but was now reneging. This couldn't have been further from the truth.

Though my agents offered to fully back me if I decided to walk away from the production, they also offered a more rational option. In their opinion, because the series was scheduled for Sunday evenings, the scenes with the most graphic nudity wouldn't be allowed by British television censors. They suggested that I take the risk and continue with my role. I might have to film the scenes which would be traumatic enough for me, but they felt certain the scenes would never be aired. I reluctantly agreed and hoped that they would be proved right.

Poldark

When I arrived in Cornwall, my frosty relationship with Tucker got even colder. He treated me terribly, refusing to speak to me. He didn't say a single word during rehearsals or filming. I dreaded the idea of having to film naked in front of cast and crew, but all of them were very sweet. The set was closed and the cameraman went to extra lengths to allow me to see what angles were being filmed and what the shots looked like. The one promise that Roger Tucker had made to me was that when we filmed these scenes, all the television monitors in the make-up and production facilities would be turned off. I later learned that he didn't keep his word, and I still am angered by his broken promise. It was the lovely Ralph Bates, cast as George Warleggan, sitting in makeup who insisted that the monitors be switched off.

Despite the uncomfortable nature of these scenes, my agents' theories proved to be spot-on. The program aired on Sunday evenings at 7:30 p.m., a prime family-viewing time slot, and all the scenes with frontal nudity were censored, leaving only one in which my naked backside was in full view as I slipped into a bathtub. The press took the opportunity to sensationalize my character's brief nudity; one of the Sunday newspapers jabbed me with the headline: "Stripper Julie Sheds Her Halo."

Nevertheless, I survived this unpleasantness and it was soon forgotten. Many of my fellow cast members have gone on to have hugely successful careers. Kevin McNally has appeared with Johnny Depp in the "Pirates of the Caribbean" films and Christopher Biggins, my love interest in the series, is also known for his roles in the *Rocky Horror Picture Show* and won the title of King of the Jungle in *I'm a Celebrity, Get Me Out of Here* in 2008. Trudie Styler married Sting, and Jane Wymark who played my sister Morwenna, has had a long standing role as John Nettle's wife in Midsomer Murders.

Opposite, left: My love interest in *Poldark* and very close friend, Christopher Biggins.

Opposite, right: With Malcolm Tierney who played Monk Adderley in the BBC series *Poldark*.

Right: A candid photo of Winston Graham the author of *Poldark*.

Gene in the classic children's tale, *The Little Prince* (1974). Our cameraman for *Willy Wonka*, Paul Wilson, joined forces with Gene to bring this sweet and touching tale to life onscreen. Seeing Gene again in later film roles was like being reunited with an old friend.

The Fox

DEEP, REFLECTIVE, THOUGHTFUL, overwhelming and profound—No question, it was a moving experience seeing Gene
in all his splendor on the screen again. *The Little Prince* and
Young Frankenstein were released in 1974, and *Silver Streak* costarring Richard Pryor, in 1976. In the presence of his characters, I felt as
though I had been reunited with an old and very close friend. His gentle nature and quirky personality opened a floodgate of emotions and memories
of our work together. I thought of my friends Peter, Denise, Paris, Roy, and
Jack and had a sense of lost youth. I was now an adult, but Gene seemed
almost unchanged onscreen. In *The Little Prince*, Gene's musical number
had the energy and charisma of his Wonka character. The book's author,
Antoine de Saint Exupéry, was an aviator who penned his magical tale from
the point of view of a pilot stranded in the Sahara desert. The enchanting
tale was only partly fiction. In 1935, Saint Exupéry and his navigator had
crashed in the Sahara desert with just a small ration of food and supplies.
After finishing *Le Petit Prince* (*The Little Prince*) and seeing it published
in 1943, Saint Exupéry joined a European squadron to help support the
Allies. His final assignment was to collect intelligence on German troop

175

Gene as Dr. Frederick Frankenstein in the unforgettable comedy *Young Frankenstein* (1974), one of his signature film collaborations with famed writer and director Mel Brooks. Screenwriter David Seltzer would later comment that it was Gene's brilliant performance and his ability to make a frightening character 'loveable' that has endeared him to audiences over the years.

movements in the south of France. On July 31, 1944, he flew into the sunset in his P-38 Lightning and was never seen or heard from again. *The Little Prince* became his legacy.

It is a touching film that remains in the hearts of its audience. I would later learn that Gene's powerful portrayal of loss reflected the news of his father's passing, which he learned of on the very day of filming.

"It is only with the heart that one can see clearly; what's essential is invisible to the eye."

Seeing Gene again in his films would touch my heart.

Gene starred in the Mel Brooks classic *Blazing Saddles*.

My wedding to my first husband Peter Mellor. Left to right: my grandmother, mother, niece Lucy Mansfield, sister Lynn, young bridesmaid Victoria Williamson, Peter, my aunt Carol Mitchell and my cousin Christopher in Hampshire (1981).

Love and Marriage

IN 1979, my romance with Peter Phipps was to end. As my career was progressing upwards, his was not doing so well at this particular time. Whilst he might be a great communicator with music, he was not so great with words and we began to drift apart. We were very young and I didn't know what was wrong, which meant I didn't know how to put it right. Believing that he was about to break off our relationship, I preempted this by getting in first. It was an incredibly sad time and he still remains my first true love.

I moved out of our little cottage and went to live with my actress friend Kate O'Mara where we shared a flat for well over a year. Television work was still prolific, but to my surprise I became ill. I lost weight and was struggling to function and keep up with work commitments. Living without my mother to take care of me, I didn't realize how ill I had become. One weekend after filming, I was so exhausted I went to bed on a Friday evening, and did not wake until late Sunday. At this point I knew I had to do something, but it was some months before I was finally diagnosed with the early onset of Tuberculosis. After a long period of treatment, I fully recovered, but all the way through, had managed to keep my career going.

With my niece Lucy Mans-
field on my wedding day
(1981).

My mother and I on my
wedding day in 1981.

Being without a father to give me away at my wedding, my dear friend and fellow actor Christopher Biggins stepped in and played a new role in my life (1981).

In 1981 I married for the first time. My husband was not an actor and the marriage was to last only seven years. Though my role in *Willy Wonka* was a big part of my youth, other than a passing comment, it was something the two of us never discussed. At this stage of my life, it had become a personal experience from my childhood rather than something revered by the public.

I Want it Now!

By 1982, I had appeared in more than twenty television features, from serious drama to comedy. Among them were many reminders of my association with Roald Dahl. *Tales of the Unexpected* was a popular British television series dramatizing a series of short stories written by Dahl, and I took the central role of Emma in the episode "The Skeleton Key." My work schedule remained hectic during this period as I continued performing in a variety of stage and television features. I had also appeared in a critically acclaimed daytime soap, *Emmerdale Farm*. The series was set in the fictional village of Emmerdale in West Yorkshire, and dramatized life in a small village and the families who lived and ran the farms. I played Pip Coulter, an adventurous runaway who at times sported a sawn-off shotgun—a nice girl led astray through association with a rough-natured boy.

In 1982, I appeared as Emma in an episode entitled *The Skeleton Key*. This was part of a series *Tales of the Unexpected* based on Roald Dahl's published short stories. The series was extremely popular in the U.K. and included performances by many popular television personalities of that era.

In period costume with actress Pippa Guard for the BBC series *Mill on the Floss* (1978) based on the original novel by George Eliot.

Sharing a light moment with actor Patrick Cargill in the LWT series "The Many Wives of Patrick."

Above: Reunited with Roy Kinnear, Sue Breen (my chaperone for *Willy Wonka*) and Bobby Roe (Peter Ostrum's stand-in and the son of Assistant Director Jack Roe) during one of Roy's performances in London, November 1978. This had represented the first and the last time I would see Sue after the completion of filming. She passed away some years later after a long battle with cancer.

Below: Over the years, I crossed paths with Roy on a variety of occasions including here at a celebrity television game show in 1978. From L-R: the actor Bryan Marshall, Christopher Biggins (my close friend and fellow cast member from *Poldark*), Roy, Christopher Blake (a fellow actor from *Mill on the Floss*), Caroline Cox (the wife of Brian Cox who played the "Dr. Hannibal Lecter" character in the 1986 film *Manhunter*), Jack Wild (of the "Artful Dodger" fame), and Jack Hedley (a very prominent actor in British film and television).

Love and Marriage

In my own life, things were more complicated. During one of my theater engagements, performing in *Mother Goose* at Bromley, I was summoned for an important phone call. In response to my tentative "Hello?" came the voice of a stranger: "Hello, Julie, it's Dad…" I had not talked to my father since he'd left when I was six, and I stood there in shock. This was the only time we would ever speak; I never saw my father, and a few years later, learned of his death in 1985. It was the end of a very sad story for all of us.

Performing with my longtime friend and fellow actor Christopher Biggins (dressed as a woman) during a pantomime performance of *Mother Goose* at Cambridge. We joke that he has been many things to me, including lover, father and now mother. Not many people can claim such a variety of roles!

As character Hilda Gittens along with actor John Duttine in the British television saga *People Like Us*. A 1920's drama series that follows several families in the London suburbs coming to terms with progressive post war culture.

Love and Marriage

In 1986, my marriage dissolved, but I continued to immerse myself in television and theater work. In 1988, I starred with Aubrey Woods in *A Tale of Two Cities*, the dramatization of the Charles Dickens classic, set in London and Paris during the French Revolution. Aubrey had played Bill the Candy Man in *Willy Wonka* and we often reminisced about our experiences. In a summer theater production, I worked with another *Willy Wonka* alumnus, Tim Brooke-Taylor, who had played the computer operator in one of the short Golden-Ticket-search scenes. Tim appeared in the last segment filmed, and when he arrived at the studio, the halls were filled with suitcases—everyone was anxious to wrap and head back to Hollywood for post-production. His scenes were rushed, which was no doubt unsatisfying. Tim and I were cast as lovers in this stage production, and I often teased him that not long before, I had been just a child. It was all in good fun.

When I finished the stage productions with Aubrey and Tim, I rushed to London to play in a comedy revival, *Dry Rot*. It was during this engagement that I met a talented comic actor who had been cast in the role of the village idiot. Nick Wilton and I developed a close friendship and not long

Acting in the stage production of *The Browning Version* by Terence Rattigan, along with fellow actors Paul Eddington, Simon Shepherd (playing my husband) and Dorothy Tutin.

Opposite and this page: In 1984, on stage at the Churchill Theatre in Bromley, Kent, starring in the theatrical comedy *The School for Wives*, written by the 17th century French playwright Molière. I played Agnès opposite Terry Scott, a well admired comedy actor well known to the British public. Getting to perform in such beautiful costumes designed by Terry Parsons was a treat. The contrast of my pale pink silk dress against the black and white Hogarth inspired scenery was stunning and this costume remains my favorite of my entire career.

Above and opposite: Christopher Biggins was cast as my love interest in the BBC series *Poldark* and we developed a close friendship that has endured the test of time. We went on to work together in a variety of stage production including this *Christmas Pantomime* (Newcastle, 1982).

Performing in a West End production with famed British Actor John Duttine another Terence Rattigan stage play entitled *Harlequinade*.

Below and opposite: Performing in various Pantomime productions during the 1980s.

This page and opposite: Playing "Titania" in William Shakespeare's *A Midsummer Night's Dream* at the Regents Park Open Air Theatre in London (1983). The character "Bottom" was played Berwick Kaler, and "Oberon" by Peter Woodward, the son of actor Edward Woodward who appeared in the 1973 classic film *The Wicker Man*.

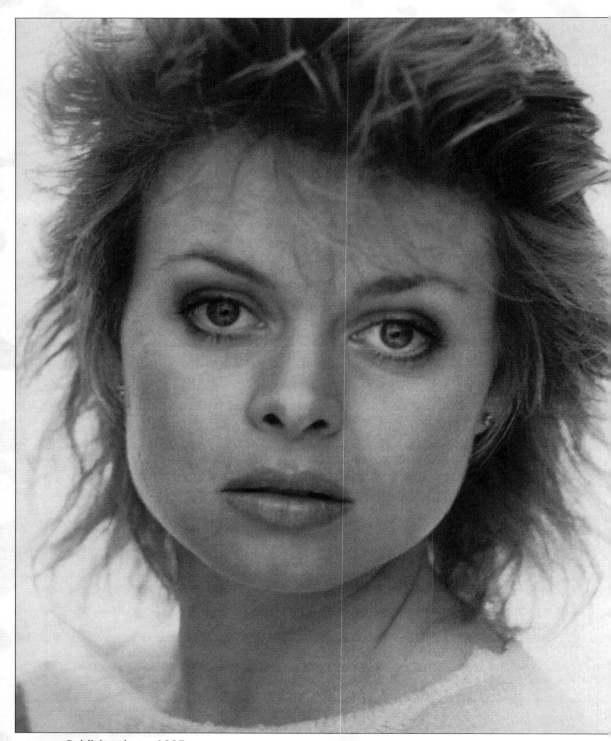

Publicity photo, 1987.

after, fell in love. We soon married and began our family. Once I became pregnant, I realized that acting was going to be a challenge. After exploring my options, I found what seemed to be a perfect fit and entered a new career phase: voice-over work. I fell in love with this type of performing; not only did it pay well, it offered schedule flexibility that wasn't possible with traditional acting work. I became the voice of products ranging from suntan lotion to cereal, I also did documentary narrations for the Discovery Channel. Amongst others, I was the voice of British Airways' automated long-haul flight announcements, bank phone systems, pharmaceutical ads, and endless television commercials.

After my beautiful daughter Holly was born in 1989, Nick and I moved our small family into the quiet community of Hampton Court. My wonderful son Barney was born in May 1993, and my husband continued acting in both stage and television while I focused mostly on voice-overs, with occasional acting roles. Little did I know that I would soon be revisiting the past...

Greeting Prince Charles during a fund raising gala with fellow actor Kenneth Branagh in 1987.

DRY ROT

by John Chapman

Cast in order of appearance

COLONEL WAGSTAFF	**RICHARD VERNON**
MRS WAGSTAFF	**ELSPET GRAY**
BETH	**JULIE PEASGOOD**
SUSAN WAGSTAFF	**JULIE DAWN COLE**
JOHN DANBY	**ROBERT BATHURST**
FRED PHIPPS	**NICK WILTON**
ALFRED TUBBE	**BRIAN RIX**
FLASH HARRY	**DEREK GRIFFITHS**
ALBERT POLIGNAC	**DEREK ROYLE**
SERGEANT FIRE	**HARRIET REYNOLDS**
COMMENTATOR	**ROBERT BATHURST**

UNDERSTUDIES

MRS WAGSTAFF, SERGEANT FIRE	**ANGELA SAUL**
POLIGNAC, FRED	**ANDREW FETTES**
BETH, SUSAN	**KATRINA SMITH**
JOHN DANBY	**ANDREW DOVE**
COMPANY AND STAGE MANAGER	**KENNETH KEYTE**
DEPUTY STAGE MANAGER	**PENELOPE FOXLEY**
ASSISTANT STAGE MANAGERS	**ANDREW DOVE**
	KATRINA SMITH
WARDROBE MISTRESS	**LAILA EMMS**

The play takes place in the lounge hall of the BULL AND COW, a country hotel.

ACT I

Scene 1   The lounge hall, morning

Scene 2   The same, three days later

ACT II

Scene 1   The same, the early hours of the following morning

Scene 2   The same, eight hours later

Scene 3   The same, that afternoon

There will be one interval of fifteen minutes

For **Lee Menzies Limited**

Production Administrator   Joanne Howes
Advertising and Graphics   Dewynters Limited 01 408 2251
Press Representative   Peter Thompson Associates
01 436 5991

Credits

Set built and painted by Victor Mara Limited
Stunts co-ordinated by Stuart St. Paul
Soda-syphons kindly donated by Schweppes

For **DRY ROT**

Production Manager   Robert Knight
Sound   Rick Clarke for the Sound
Department Ltd
Production Electrician   Bill Wardropper
Property Buyer   Jane Slattery
Costume Supervisor   Kim Baker
Assistant to Tim Goodchild   David Shields
Production Photographer   John Haynes

In 1993 with my newborn son Barney and daughter Holly.

My wedding day with Nick Wilton, my step father Alan Kinnair and my Mother.

Nick and me with Holly in 1989.

Celebrating my close friend Fern Britton's 50th birthday along with her co-host from ITV's *This Morning*, Phillip Schofield, and my daughter Holly.

A New Chapter

ASWARM OF CONFLICTS followed the theatrical release of *Willy Wonka and the Chocolate Factory*, but they seemed to help more than hurt the film. Among them were a variety of licensing issues arising from the property rights still owned by Quaker Oats. Additionally, Roald Dahl—frustrated by the final film version—refused to sell the sequel rights, which influenced Paramount Pictures' decision not to renew its distribution contract. The rights were finally optioned to Warner Brothers, opening a new chapter in the film's saga.

In the early 1980s, video was quickly becoming the standard in home entertainment. Warner Brothers believed in the film's nostalgic potential, and more than a decade after its release, *Willy Wonka and the Chocolate Factory* was enjoying a mass following through new matinee theater engagements, television broadcasts, and home video sales. The film also became popular in foreign markets, with new audio tracks dubbed in a variety of languages.

When my daughter Holly was about five, I decided it was time to share with her the magic of what had played such an important part of my life. As the opening credits rolled and the well-loved music filled the room, Holly dozed unimpressed.

My mother attended my graduation ceremony at Greenwich University in 2009 which was sadly to be our last family outing. It was incredibly special to have her with me to celebrate such a momentous day. I know she has always been proud of me but that day was special.

During this same period, I found myself re-examining my life. My marriage to Nick had fallen apart and I decided it was time to start a new chapter. Working as an actor often required living out of a suitcase, and as a single parent, this was not a viable way to raise my children. Dance and aerobics were among the array of theatrical arts that I'd studied, and during travel and between shooting schedules, I spent a lot of time in the gym, staying in shape. On occasion, I had been asked to lead some of the aerobics classes. Finally, my local gym suggested that I consider becoming a qualified fitness instructor myself. This sounded like a great opportunity for me to pursue something I really enjoyed and it would keep a roof over our heads. I qualified as a fitness instructor in 1999. I took classes and also clients for personal training. When a friend at ITV found out about my new career, I was recruited to be an expert on a British television reality program, *Fat Families*.

This created an entirely new role for me in network television. I became the fitness expert on the popular daytime show *This Morning*, shown on ITV. One of my first adventures was to travel with program host Fern Britton to Egypt, where we filmed a daily diary while doing a charity cross-country bicycle ride along the banks of the Nile. It was a fantastic experience and yielded a similar program the following year. *The Challenge of Your Life*, focused on ten women taking on extreme challenges. My job was to train and mentor them all. Two women would join Fern and myself cycling though India, four women would run the London Marathon and the remaining four, would swim the English Channel to France. Being part of this program has been one of the most fulfilling journeys of my lifetime. Fern and I have become very good friends both on- and off-screen, and our adventures continue.

Another byproduct of the fitness training was my interest in psychoanalysis. Over time, I've become increasingly interested in human psychology and the connection between emotional and physical health. This interest opened yet another door and influenced my return to academia to become a psychotherapist. I graduated in October 2009, with a degree in Humanistic Counseling, and no one was prouder than my mother who attended the ceremony at Greenwich University. Sadly it was to be her last outing...

I remain fascinated by the unconscious conflicts and methods of interpreting and resolving problems of this nature. At this point, I don't know where this path will take me, but my work with clients, helping them identify how their unconscious often manifests itself in ways that make them their own worst enemies, has proven to be some of the most rewarding I've ever done. Who knows how Veruca Salt would have turned out had she had psychotherapy?

Left: A family portrait of Barney, Holly and me taken in 2001.

Right: My daughter Holly at matriculation for Girton College (Cambridge 2008).

Rob Newman, who was the roughly the same age as us child actors, was a common presence on the set of *Willy Wonka*. We have always considered him as one of us Wonka kids. Rob's father was a well-known Hollywood executive and was hired to represent Quaker Oats, the principle financier of *Willy Wonka and the Chocolate Factory*. Having served as the Vice President for Samuel Goldwyn Studios and later working for Howard Hughes' Production Company, he brought an unprecedented caliber of expertise to the table and often visited the set to ensure things were running smoothly (not to mention that he co-signed every check used for payment during the production since he had ultimate responsibility for representing Quakers' interests and final budget oversight). But behind the scenes, Rob's father had a much more crucial role ... Rob and his father lived next door to the Dahl's in Los Angeles in the early 60's, and had maintained an extremely close relationship with both Roald and his wife Patricia Neal (a renowned actress of the era). The production principles leveraged this bond, and looked upon Newman as both a liaison and mediator of sorts; to essentially smooth over the political conflicts occurring between Dahl and the filmmakers. During the making of the movie the Newman's would travel from Munich to Dahl's home in England and meet. For me personally, Rob and his father remained very dear friends and whenever they came to London I'd join them for tea. Even following his father's death, Rob and I have continued our friendship, meeting frequently all over the world. I consider myself lucky to experience such a lasting friendship.

"A Thing of Beauty Is a Joy Forever..."

THERE WAS ONE LINK to *Willy Wonka* that I never lost—my enduring friendship with Rob Newman, son of Quaker Oats principal and an executive producer of *Willy Wonka*, Bob Newman. As a child, Rob was a fixture on the set, and we became close both during and after the production. When he and his father came to England, they would always invite me to the Dorchester Hotel for tea. It was Rob's father who had become devastated when he learned that my mother had paid her own way to see me during my birthday and later made sure she was reimbursed for her travel.

Rob's ties to Hollywood run deep. His family linage includes an impressive ensemble of maverick filmmakers, producers and composers. Their legacies are still today the pillars of Hollywood. His father had been the Vice President of Samuel Goldwyn Studios and later went on to become 'Head of Production' for Howard Hughes who produced films from the 1920's until 1957. His mother had also been recruited by Hughes to train as an actress and though both never made any pictures under Hughes, Rob's father traveled the world to sell syndication rights from Hughes' library of epic films.

His father later went on to represent Quaker Oats, the financier of *Willy Wonka*, and it was this association that we developed a deep friendship that has lasted over four decades.

Rob, who has continued his family heritage as prominent producer, still owns several important artifacts from the production (not to mention one of Howard Hughes's homes). Our mutual love for the film has kept us close for years— myself and the others often refer to him as the honorary *Wonka* kid. It was Rob who kept me up to date on the other cast members and how they were doing.

In 1997, Gene Crowell, a major *Willy Wonka* fan, started tracking down my fellow cast members and began working to reunite us for a collector's convention in New York. Thanks to Gene's diligent leg-work, reunion plans started coming together. I was so thrilled, and couldn't wait to see everyone; the prospect of meeting each again and reliving our memories seemed like pure magic. Though Michael and Denise weren't able to attend, Peter Ostrum , Paris Themmen and myself would participate. I was utterly thrilled.

When we arrived at the convention, we were escorted to a table with tons of *Wonka* memorabilia and the movie playing on a continuous loop. The convention was filled with film and television personalities from the golden era through the 1970s, many of whom were heroes from my own childhood. It was extraordinary on so many levels. When Peter entered the room, I recognized him almost immediately. His features had softened into those of a distinguished gentleman, but it was his voice that took me back to my youth. Peter Ostrum was now Dr. Ostrum. By his own choice, he never acted again after leaving the *Wonka* set. When he returned home, his family bought a horse and Peter began working at the stable where the horse was boarded. His love for the horse and the gentle nature of the horse's veterinarian inspired him to pursue a career in veterinary medicine; he graduated in 1984 from the College of Veterinary Medicine at Cornell University. He now practices in rural upstate New York, and on occasion, visits public schools to talk about *Willy Wonka*, what it's like to be a veterinarian, and how one's life changes with the decisions one makes. Peter came to the convention with his wife, Loretta, his son, Leif, and his daughter, Helinka.

When Paris arrived, it was as though we were back to our childhoods. Paris was still in many ways, Paris; no longer obnoxious, but still mischievous and

Above: Reunited with Peter and Paris in 1997 at an autograph convention in New Jersey. This was the first time we'd seen each other since saying our good-byes in Germany. It wasn't until I met some of the devoted Wonka fans at this convention that I recognized the sheer magnitude of *Willy Wonka's* cultural resonance.

Right: Peter Ostrum and I at the Hal-loween themed "Chiller Convention" in New Jersey (1997). I couldn't resist join-ing in and had a pair of vampire fangs costume made.

energetic. He lives in Los Angeles, and has traveled the globe as an entrepre-neur of world-class proportions. We talked for hours, catching up on all the years—more than 25—since we had last seen each other. Public reception was also awe-inspiring. Lines seemed endless as we signed photos, movie cases, Wonka bars, and every imaginable kind of movie memorabilia.

Our full cast reunion including Director Mel Stuart was organized by our friend and *Wonka* fan Gene Crowell in Boston (1998). It was wonderful for us all to meet again for the first time in nearly thirty years.

Dinner that evening was enjoyable and heartwarming. Joined by Rob Newman, we laughed endlessly, telling our stories about the production and everything *Wonka*. There were also somber moments when we reminisced fondly about Jack Albertson and Roy Kinnear, both of whom had since passed away. Jack died in 1981 following a long bout with cancer, and my dear Roy had also died tragically at only 54 while filming with his longtime friend, Richard Lester. Roy had been on location in Spain filming *The Return of the Musketeers* when he fell from a horse and sustained a broken pelvis. He was taken to a hospital in Madrid and died unexpectedly the following day. It was devastating to everyone who knew and loved him. It was especially hard for Richard Lester, who never made another film. Roy, the closest I had to a real father during that part of my life, was laid to rest in a cemetery close to where I grew up in Surrey.

What we took from the convention was something I hadn't realized: *Willy Wonka and the Chocolate Factory* had endeared itself to so many people of so many different ages. It seemed to have touched everyone, both young and old. We talked with people for hours upon hours about how important the film was to them.

The next convention was scheduled the following year in Boston, and the event was to be the first time all of the "*Wonka* kids" would be together. Unbeknownst to one another, both Denise and I arrived at Boston's Logan Airport at about the same time and were picked up by the same livery service. I didn't recognize her at first, but when she spoke, everything came back. We talked for hours and caught up on our lives. Mel Stuart, Michael Böllner (Augustus Gloop), Rusty Goffe (one of the Oompa Loompas) and Diana Sowle (Mrs. Bucket) were also present for the reunion. Michael now spoke excellent English and all us were able to communicate with him.

Mel hadn't changed much—he easily fell back into his directing role, orchestrating each of our positions during a photo shoot as well as our seating arrangements at dinner. It was as though we were on the set of *Willy Wonka* again, nervously reverting to our childhood roles under his direction.

The following morning, as we were driving to the autograph convention, Diana leaned over to me and said, "I don't know why we're all so nervous around Mel; he can't fire us now…" We laughed and laughed, telling story after story of those magical experiences in the Bavarian Studios.

In a limousine traveling to a Manhattan studio to record the audio commentary for the Warner Brothers 30th Anniversary DVD release. This also represented the first time all of the "*Wonka* kids" sat together in the same room to watch the film.

T HE FOLLOWING YEAR, Warner Brothers decided to celebrate the thirtieth anniversary of the film's release with a special remastered version, which was to include a retrospective documentary with cast commentary. Since all of the kid actors would be together for a reunion at another convention in New York, Warner Brothers hired a producer to meet us there and do the individual interviews. Following the convention, we would be driven to a production studio where we would watch the film together for the first time and record the audio commentary. The producers, who had already been conducting interviews in Los Angeles with Mel Stuart, David Wolper, and David Seltzer, flew to New York to meet with Peter, Paris, Denise, Michael, and me. The day after our interviews, they would travel to Gene Wilder's home in Connecticut to record his memories.

The schedule for the New York convention was intense. We each undertook separate interviews for the documentary in the morning before the convention, and then were driven to a production studio in Manhattan to record the commentary that evening. Warner Brothers hired a limousine to drive all of us from our hotel to the production studio. After a long and full day of meeting with fans, we were all fairly exhausted. Nonetheless, we enjoyed the food and beverages that awaited us in the limousine. As we traveled across the Manhattan Bridge, accompanied by the song "Who Let the Dogs Out," on the radio, we sang our hearts out childishly as if we were all thirteen again. It was lovely! When the car pulled up to the studio entrance, the driver opened the door and out rolled beer bottles in every direction. Not quite the wholesome kids we once were… It was great fun sitting together for the first time watching the film. Words can't describe the experience we shared, watching it together, reliving those moments from our past.

I had a chance meeting with Gene Wilder during the same year. While on a promotional tour in Europe, he was a special guest on ITV's *This Morning Show*, the program on which I was a contributor as the resident fitness expert. I was invited to make a surprise appearance in the studio. It was thrilling to see him again after so many years. We both enjoyed hearing one another's memories of the production, and he seemed to be the same Gene from years earlier. During a commercial break, he leaned over to me and whispered in his soft voice, "I guess Veruca wasn't such a bad egg after all." We spoke backstage for a brief period, and with a hug, said goodbye.

In 2003, all of the Wonka kids were reunited back in Germany to visit the various locations where *Willy Wonka* was filmed. It was a deeply profound experience for all of us. There we stood again at the gates of *Wonka's* chocolate factory, reflecting on how a part of this important film had changed the course of all our lives. The landscape and much of the architecture had changed and some areas were barely recognizable. The cement pathway that led to the magical factory had crumbled away and was now grown-over with grass and foliage. But standing there, peering deep into the landscape moved us all. For one brief moment in time, we did the impossible; we traveled back to our childhoods as if we had never left. It all began at this very gate...More than thirty years had since passed, and we had now come full circle...

"Round the World and Home Again...
That's the Sailor's Way!"

IN 2002, the *Wonka* kids met once more, but this time it was back in Germany, where we were invited by a documentary film team to record our memories on-camera. We revisited the film studios, and the exteriors of the buildings seemed unchanged, though of course, the interiors reflected current productions. But the massive Chocolate Room still had a certain atmosphere about it. All of us ventured into different areas and reflected on how our experiences there had changed our lives.

Once again, we stayed at the Schloss Hotel and again laughed for hours as we told stories. We walked along the river together, with Peter still trying to teach Denise and myself the art of skipping stones, just as he had done during our youth. I have to say with the same lack of success. I even remembered the sad walk back to the tram station when I had said goodbye to my mother and sister, and the memory brought with it a flood of tears. But the most vivid memory came inside the Schloss Hotel: the odd spacing of the hotel's stairs, which I had traversed hundreds of times during the filming had not changed.

On the last day of our visit, a cold and snowy February morning, the five of us returned to the main gate of the Munich Gas Works where it had all begun. Adults now and together again at that gate for the first time since we had filmed those scenes, we embraced one another at the entrance to Willy Wonka's factory. It was a profound and moving moment for each of us. There were new buildings and changes in some of the architecture, but the outline of Wonka's factory was still there. We looked deep into the land-scape as though expecting Gene to reappear in costume.

This was where it all started for me. My first scenes on film happened at the very place I was standing. I closed my eyes and could hear Roy whisper-ing that special poem to me, and recalled the magic of seeing Gene Wilder emerge as Willy Wonka for the first time. It was as though I had traveled back to that pivotal day.

The Legacy of Veruca Salt

I'S SOMETIMES HARD to fathom that Veruca, despite her flaws, has remained in the hearts of so many people worldwide. As I travel, I'm always pleasantly surprised when I reveal my Veruca identity and out comes that gasp of "Oh my God!" This phenomenon was well illustrated by the clever Australian comedian, Matthew Hardy. In 2004, I received an email from my agent about an interview request by Hardy. As it turned out, Hardy was a *Wonka* nut. He had been obsessed with the film since first seeing it as a child and his fascination led to him write a comedic show, *Searching for Veruca Salt*. This production, which debuted at the Melbourne International Comedy Festival, follows Hardy as an adult in therapy, attempting to come to terms with his obsession with Veruca Salt. The promotional trailer captures its witty flavor:

At the age of five, he fell in love… At the age of thirty-five, he finally did something about it. We see Matthew in Australia and Julie in England sitting on their respective therapist's couches. Matthew is complaining about his constant obsession with a film he saw when he was five years old…. Julie complains about the obsession from fans over a movie she was in over thirty years ago. Four women had dumped Matthew over a ten-year time span, and in each case it was due in part to his continued fascination with the Veruca Salt character from the original Willy Wonka and the Chocolate Factory film . . .

I was originally invited to help promote the show at the opening of the festival, but ever up for a challenge, I thought it would be fun to be in it myself. After all, who could do it better than me? It was a great deal of fun, and the show was a hit with the audiences. I met scores of people who had long treasured *Willy Wonka* and so enjoyed hearing their stories and what the film had meant to them. The experience proved not only powerful for Matthew, but for me as well.

As the festival drew near its close, Matthew took me to see the very movie theater in which he had watched *Willy Wonka* as a child. There was something about standing in front of that theater—it was one of those powerful experiences that seemed to bring me full circle.

Holly, Barney and myself with Matthew Hardy in his Willy Wonka costume for the stage production of *Willy Wonka Explained—The Veruca Salt Sessions* during Melbourne Comedy Festival in Australia (2004).

With friends during our annual crazy New Year's celebration in Angmering on England's South Coast (2004).

Taking in some of the local cuisine and cultural traditions during my three weeks in Melbourne, Australia (for Matthew Hardy's production).

Happily Ever After...

AFTER SO MANY DECADES, I still look back and marvel at how *Willy Wonka and the Chocolate Factory* has endured. And despite some of the tragedies and hardships, offset by many triumphs that I've come to embrace over my lifetime, there is little question that my life was forever changed after passing through those gates of the Munich Gas Works in September 1970. It is worlds apart from the realities of my own life today, but when I watch the movie, I can still feel the magic and the excitement in the eyes of that little girl who had been through so much at that young age. But life was just beginning.

There are still many roads un-traveled in my life, and I intend to keep exploring each and every one. I'm proud of the legacy we left for future generations and how it has touched the lives of so many people. In my own small way, I may even have directly encouraged others to follow in my footsteps. In 1997, I founded my own Saturday morning theatre school for children, Centerstage in Surrey. It's been great to see my young pupils experience the same fun and creativity that ignited my career all those years ago. It's been nice to be able put something back and encourage others the way that I was encouraged. I don't expect them all to become performers, but the skills they have learned set them up for life.

Over the years, I've heard countless stories from fans telling me how the movie helped them through difficult times, or was the cautionary tale they used to instill morals into their children. But no one has been more inspired or has more love for the film than I. It has become part of the fabric of who I am. My children are still exploring their own paths in life, but all of us have been forever changed by that extraordinary tale of Charlie Bucket.

But the story had a flaw. You see, I actually found two Golden Tickets: my children Holly and Barney. They are my lifetime of unconditional love and happiness.

"If you want to view paradise, simply look around..."

I can still hear that magical music.

I don't believe that any of us back in 1970 could imagine the impact and influence *Willy Wonka* would have on our lives. An experience as everlasting as Mr. Wonka's legendary Gob-stoppers. A timeless, ageless story that ends happily ever after...

Acknowledgments

THIS IS MY CHANCE to tell all of the important people in my life how much I love them and value their friendships. I always read these dedications in books and wonder who the people mentioned are. Well, this is my chance to have my say...

So in no particular order, my dearest friend Patricia Shakesby who has always been there for me, Godmother to Holly India, and the most loyal friend. Colette Gleeson, to whom I shall always be "baby," and has given my children and I the best and happiest times of our lives, and given me the family that I would have wanted. To all those at 'Angmering', Cheers! Carolyne Cross, whom I consider a sister! Love you Carolyne! xxx. Fern Britton for all the fun and adventure we have had -Thelma to my Louise, and not forgetting all the other Panda girls, Val Colley, Donna Barry, Charlotte Thompson and Juliet Borges. Pandas rule! Norman and Sheila Mann, dear, dear friends and Godparents to Barney, as well as being my honorary parents! Tim Bond, who played so beautifully for my mother's service, and is one of the most talented guys I know, and all my CenterStagers, especially the beautiful Ali Pyne! (Oh yes you are!) Dianne Nelmes, what can I say? Friend, confidante and always there. Crazy Debbie, I'll never lose weight while you're around! Richard &

225

Sue Buswell, who shared a very special time with me and my mum, and many others over the years. Karen & Pearse Lehane, such lovely friends and I am so happy to have been partly responsible for getting you together. Tony Suttile, who gave me the chance to have special time with my kids; a big guy with a big heart. Tracie Rice, love and light Tracie! Leo Kenny, whom I've known for so many years, and still makes me smile. You owe me a beer Leo! Always here. And Alan Kinnair, a stepfather who cherished and cared for my mother to the end. She was lucky to have you, and I am lucky to have you as my stepfather.

Special thanks also goes to the extraordinary designers John Reinhardt (interior), Jim Zach (cover) and Joshua Tallent (ebook); Susan Tasaki (editor); curator Sona Basmadjian for the "David L. Wolper Center for the Study of the Documentary" at the University of Southern California, and publisher Ben Ohmart from BearManor Media.

It goes without saying that I have to acknowledge my Wonka 'brothers & sisters'; and of course Wonkerers everywhere. Gene Crowell, my buddy in DC without whom none of the Wonka 'kids' would be reunited. You may be a fan, but I count you and Amy as my friends, first and foremost, and without you the journey of the last few years would not have happened. Thanks Gene.

Finally, I would like to thank Michael Esslinger, without whose enthusiasm, hard work and support this project would never have got off the ground. I always felt there was a story to be told, but didn't know where to start. Michael gave it a voice.

But more importantly, he provided me with a unique gift for my mother. Michael and I had been collaborating for some months, and finally we had a draft version. I gave this to my mother to read in January 2010, not realizing that these were to be her final days. She loved it . . .

What an incredible thing it must have been for a mother to get the chance to reflect on her daughter's life, and to know that as my mother she was loved without reservation and unequivocally. We don't all get the chance to tell our mothers that. My mother passed away on 3rd Feb 2010. An extraordinary woman who gave me an extraordinary life.

So I will forever be indebted to Michael, and know that this story will forever bond me to him, and his lovely family, Julie, Forrest, Brandon and Ross.

"We are the music makers and we are the dreamers of dreams."

Index

Index

About the Authors

JULIE DAWN COLE is an English television, film and stage actress with a prolific career in show business spanning over four decades. She began as a child performer in what remains one of her best-remembered roles as the spoiled Veruca Salt in Roald Dahl's *Willy Wonka & the Chocolate Factory*. She has appeared in hundreds of broadcast, film and stage productions and became a household name for her work in many popular British television series. Julie lives in Surrey, England, with her two children, Holly India, and Barnaby, Tess the dog and Lily the cat. After 40 years in show business, she is now a practicing psychotherapist working primarily with children and young adults.

MICHAEL ESSLINGER is a historical researcher and best-selling author whose acclaimed work has appeared in numerous books, film and television documentaries, including segments on the Discovery, National Geographic and History Channels. His work spans entertainment, science, politics and historical subjects. He has interviewed icons that have shaped world history and continues to write on subjects that explore a vast spectrum of the human experience. He resides on the California Coast with his wife and three sons.

"I want it now'."

- Veruca Salt'